WINNING ON THE GROUND

TRAINING AND TECHNIQUES FOR JUDO AND MMA FIGHTERS

AnnMaria De Mars and James Pedro Sr.

WINNING ON THE GROUND

TRAINING AND TECHNIQUES FOR JUDO AND MMA FIGHTERS

AnnMaria De Mars and James Pedro Sr.

Edited by Vicki Baker and Jeannine Santiago

Graphic Design by John Bodine

Principal Photography by Peter Lueders

Additional Photos by Dennis De Mars, Hans Gutnecht,
Rick Hustead, Riley McIlwain

Second Printing 2013

WARNING

BLACK BELT BOOKS
A Division of OHARA PUBLICATIONS, INC.
World Leader in Martial Arts Publications

ABOUT THE AUTHORS

ANNMARIA DE MARS

Dr. AnnMaria De Mars was the first American to win the World Judo Championships. She is one of the most decorated U.S. *judokas* in the history of the sport.

De Mars has more than 40 years of judo experience both as an elite athlete and international coach. For more than a decade, she was one of the top female competitors in the sport. She won international gold medals on four continents, placing first at the Pan-American Games, Austrian Open, the Pacific Rim Championships, U.S. Open and the Canada Cup. Her dominance among U.S. competitors was unrivaled at the time. She was a three-time national champion, two-time junior national champion, collegiate national champion and national *sambo* wrestling champion. De Mars capped her illustrious competitive career by winning the 56-kilogram division of the 1984 World Judo Championships in Vienna. It was a feat no American man or woman had achieved before.

At 14, De Mars became an assistant judo instructor to help pay for her own lessons. In the four decades since, she has coached athletes who have won medals at every level from the junior and collegiate national levels to the international stage. She has introduced the sport to preschool judokas and has trained Olympians. She coached at Venice Dojo in California from the late 1990s through the mid-2000s, during which time Venice was the top junior club in the country. De Mars was the 2004 U.S. Judo Federation coach of the year. She established the West Coast Judo Training Center in 2008 where she coaches athletes in judo, mixed martial arts and grappling.

From 2005 to 2010, De Mars was a member of the board of directors of the U.S. Judo Association, serving as its president from 2009 to 2010.

De Mars is president and CEO of The Julia Group, a technology consulting firm. She holds a Ph.D. in educational psychology and an MBA. She resides in Santa Monica, California, with her husband, Dennis. She has four daughters, including Ronda Rousey, women's 135-pound Strikeforce champion, UFC fighter and Olympic bronze medalist. For more information about De Mars, visit thejuliagroup.com.

JAMES PEDRO SR.

James Pedro Sr.'s career in judo as a coach and competitor spans nearly five decades. He represented the United States as an international competitor in events in Europe and South America, winning the bronze medal in the Pan-American Judo Championships in Panama. He medaled five times in senior national competitions in three weight divisions, placing in the 176, 209 and open-weight categories. He also placed fifth as a member of the U.S. national team in the Pre-World competition.

Pedro's greatest accomplishments have been in coaching. His club, Pedro's Judo Center, has been producing world and Olympic medalists since 1980. He has had an athlete on every one of the last five Olympic teams. All the Olympic medals the United States won from 1996 through 2008 were brought home by players coached by Pedro, including two by his son, Jimmy Pedro Jr., and one by Ronda Rousey.

James Pedro Sr. coached the most recent U.S. male world champion (Jimmy Pedro Jr., 1999) and the most recent U.S. female world champion (Kayla Harrison, 2010). With Jimmy Jr. as the coach of Team USA, the Pedros were in London for the 2012 Olympic Games in which Harrison won gold and Marti Malloy won bronze.

In addition to his coaching accomplishments in judo, James Pedro Sr. has coached athletes to success in wrestling and mixed martial arts. Athletes in his wrestling program have won medals in state, regional and collegiate championships. Two of his players have crossed over to mixed martial arts with major success: Rick Hawn, winner of the Bellator Fighting Championships lightweight tournament, and Ronda Rousey, Strikeforce women's world champion.

PREFACE

*T**he goal is to win.*** Whether you are competing in judo, grappling or mixed martial arts, the goal is simple—to win in any way the rules allow, to avoid mistakes and jump on opportunities. The arm lock Ronda Rousey is doing on Travis McLaughlin is the one she used on her way to winning her first gold medal at the World Cup in Great Britain in 2006. This wasn't the armbar she originally intended to do in that match (as explained in Chapter 2), but when the chance was there, she took it.

Winners take advantage of opportunities to win, and a lot of those occur on the ground.

In every match, there is an instant when the gold medal is up for grabs and one person reaches out and grabs it. That scenario, replayed here by Rousey and McLaughlin, occurred in the 2008 Olympic trials. One player (in white in the bottom photo) attempted a throw. The other player stopped it by a hard hip block that ended up knocking the attacker face-first to the ground. Although this is not a score in judo, it represents a perfect opportunity to attack. Several effective ground techniques can begin from this position.

Winning opportunities come in two basic types: first, those that are likely to occur in a match, as described above; second, those you make happen by

The purpose of this book is to help you spot those opportunities to win a match on the ground and teach you ways of drilling so that your reactions are almost automatic.

causing a reaction in your opponent. This book also will teach you how to take opportunities and how to make them.

We don't believe in luck. We believe in training. Many times, people have seen us or our players win and commented that we were "lucky" to catch the arm lock, choke or pin just at the right moment. In fact, they are looking at someone doing a move that he or she has drilled thousands of times. It only looks like luck. We do drills for turnovers, drills for escapes, drills for chokes and drills for arm locks (as shown in the photo below). We also do drills for strength and conditioning.

There is no substitute for hard work. If you picked up this book hoping to find magic martial arts secrets to winning without training, you have come to the wrong place. We've had people tell us that they don't believe in training harder; they train smarter. Winning on the ground comes from training smarter *and* harder. Technique may be better than strength, but technique and strength are even better. When it comes to winning mat work, the secret is working hard doing the right things.

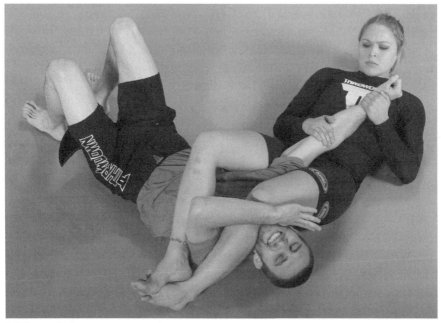

Drill for arm locks.

FOREWORD

From the modern pioneers of the American judo scene, AnnMaria De Mars and Jim Pedro Sr., comes an insightful new book any judo player should have. Building on their experiences in judo from their own heyday and groundbreaking achievements, they have had ubiquitous effects on the sport.

AnnMaria, a former world judo champion, passed the judo genetics to her daughter Ronda Rousey. Under her mother's tutelage, Ronda conquered women's judo, as well, becoming a world judo champion and medaling in the Olympics. AnnMaria continues to coach Ronda to success beyond judo. Ronda has achieved legitimate celebrity by dominating and becoming the face of the nascent sport of women's mixed martial arts.

Jim Pedro Sr., an influential and important pioneer in the sport, has been a force in American judo for decades. His son, Jimmy Pedro Jr., carried on that tradition and, with his father's guidance, became a world judo champion and twice medaled in the Olympics. Father and son cultivated and coached the next generation of American *judoka* at the pre-eminent Pedro's Judo Center in Wakefield, Massachusetts. Their efforts led to the historic 2012 Olympic Games in London where Kayla Harrison won America's first gold medal in judo. Jimmy Jr. also coached Marti Malloy to her bronze medal for Team USA Judo at the games.

American judo will forever be linked to AnnMaria De Mars and Jim Pedro Sr. Future generations of judo players will always be indebted to them.

—*Maurice Allan, MBE*
seventh *dan,* former Olympian, European wrestling champion,
seven-time Scottish National Judo champion and
FILA World Sambo Wrestling champion

CONTENTS

ABOUT THE AUTHORS 4

PREFACE 6

FOREWORD 8

CHAPTER 1
SIX "SECRETS" TO BETTER GROUND WORK:
BASIC REASONS MOST PEOPLE DON'T WIN 10

CHAPTER 2
MAT-WORK CONNECTIONS:
A DOZEN QUICK WAYS TO A SUBMISSION 25

CHAPTER 3
TWO MAT-WORK TECHNIQUES
EVERYONE SHOULD KNOW 61

CHAPTER 4
MAT-WORK SERIES:
LEAVING AN OPPONENT NOWHERE TO GO 69

CHAPTER 5
MAT-WORK COUNTERS.. 106

CHAPTER 6
DRILL THE RIGHT WAY TO WIN ON THE GROUND
(HOW TO BE DANGEROUS ON THE MAT).................................. 118

CHAPTER 7
BASIC MAT-WORK DRILL TRAINING 127

CHAPTER 8
SITUATION DRILLS.. 153

CHAPTER 9
ESSENTIALS OF WINNING ON THE GROUND 192

APPENDIX.. 196

CHAPTER 1

SIX "SECRETS" TO BETTER GROUND WORK: BASIC REASONS MOST PEOPLE DON'T WIN

It was 1983 and the first time the Pan-American Games included a women's judo division. I can't speak for the rest of the competitors, but I know I was nervous. I'd had a good run, won a lot of tournaments prior to the games, but that only made it worse. I told Dr. James Wooley, the team manager and a two-time Olympian, I was stressed because no matter how much I trained, I knew there was a possibility that I could still make a mistake in a match. He laughed and said, "You're thinking about it all wrong. You don't have to be perfect to win this tournament. You don't need to never make a mistake. You just need to go out there and in each match make one less mistake than the other person."

—AnnMaria De Mars

People can—and do—make many mistakes in mat work. We focus on building champions on the ground in part because ground work is such an overlooked part of winning for many people in judo and mixed martial arts. *Jiu-jitsu* players, on the other hand, love ground work. Their problem is usually the opposite. They overlook the standing part a bit too much, so they miss chances that happen as they move from standing to ground work.

How can you keep from making the same mistakes as everyone else? If you read nothing else in this book, read the first two sections on transition and combinations to learn how to avoid the two biggest mistakes people make. Watch any tournament and you'll see one common missed opportunity: hesitating just a split second after a throw and allowing the opponent a chance to escape. A second one is not having a backup plan for a mat technique—the opponent escapes from a technique and there's no follow-up. If your training keeps you from making those two mistakes, you'll have improved your ground work by more than 100 percent.

The six "secrets" in this chapter can improve your mat work dramatically in a short period. Then there is everything else, including having a variety of techniques, being able to attack from different positions and understanding defense. It was impossible to put more than a small number of our ideas on ground work here, so we selected a few at random, out of 100 other equally good ways to make your mat techniques better. Of course, effective armbars, transitions, mat-work combinations and the rest of the tips we include in this first chapter are just the basics of good ground work. However, we seldom see these practiced regularly in martial arts, so they might as well be secrets that are locked up somewhere.

Good mat work requires a certain "sixth sense" that comes from hours on the mat in learning techniques and doing those techniques during free practice and drills. The tips in this chapter are one way to develop that sense, and the drills in this book are another way. Most of all, there is no substitute for putting in the hours on the ground and doing mat techniques in every possible situation.

There are a lot of other tips to improve your mat work, and this chapter covers several of them. However, if you are in a rush—need to catch a plane, don't read much, are being attacked by ninjas, whatever—pay special attention to the first two.

SECRET NO. 1

TRANSITION: PLAN TO TAKE ADVANTAGE OF THAT SECOND FROM STANDING TO GROUND WORK

A player throws and there is a second or two from the throw until following up to the mat. In that second, the opponent turns on his or her stomach, rolls to the side or sits up. These split-second moves put the opponent into a little better position. Why didn't the player who threw immediately follow up to the ground? You start a match standing up. You know this. Yet, if you are like most people, you practice standing or you practice ground work, and you very seldom practice moving from one to the other.

Transition is movement from one position or state to another. On the next page, Olympic gold-medalist Kayla Harrison and Aaron Kunihiro are practicing a drill in which one person throws and then goes into a pin the second they hit the mat. We teach this kind of drill in our beginning classes, when students are just learning to do throws and hold-downs. Unfortunately, this is *not* the way most people learn mat work from the very beginning, which is why they make mistakes later on.

SECRET NO. 1: Take Advantage When You Can

During this drill, one person throws and then goes into a pin as they hit the mat.

Start thinking about mat work from the second you take a grip on your opponent. When you land, keep that grip, settle your weight onto your hips, spread your legs apart to be balanced on a strong base and get into the pin. The time from landing until a pin is called should be one second or less if the referee is paying attention. If you find yourself complaining that the referee didn't give you enough time to get your mat technique to work, you're doing it wrong. The referee shouldn't even be in the picture.

Although this first example is basic (from a throw to a pin), as you'll see in Chapter 2, it doesn't always have to be that simple. This example does show, however, that transition is something that ought to be learned from day one, not added on later. As Aristotle said, "We are what we repeatedly do. Excellence, then, is not an act but a habit." Get into the habit of transition every time you throw. If you do it enough, it should be instinctive. Instinct is the best way of doing anything.

SECRET NO. 2

TRANSITION IN MOVING BETWEEN GROUND TECHNIQUES: PLAN TO TAKE ADVANTAGE OF YOUR OPPONENT'S ATTEMPTS TO ESCAPE

Here is a drill we do that teaches mat-work counters, practicing escapes and counters to escapes. It starts with a very simple, basic move, but it quickly gets unexpected. Let's start with the move we are going to counter. Note that although this is demonstrated in judo *gi* in the photos, it can be done just as easily in a no-gi situation just by grabbing the head and the arm. This is a very common scene in mat work with really inexperienced players. The two end up on their knees facing each another. One player tries to grab the other around the neck and throws the other on her back. (In judo, when this technique is done from a standing position, it is called *koshi guruma.*)

In this drill (plans A through D), we practice a very basic turnover to a pin, a counter to that turnover into a different pin, an escape from that pin and a counter to that escape into a different pin.

SECRET NO. 2—Plan A: Head and Arm Throw to a Pin

1. Crystal Butts (in white) grabs Ronda Rousey around the head and by the right arm. Butts then turns so that her hips are in front. Butts pulls with her left hand, which has a grip on Rousey's elbow.

2. Butts continues pulling with the left arm, holding the opponent tight to her body by the grip on the head, and turning her whole body to the right.

Continued on next page

3. As Butts turns, Rousey is thrown over her hips and onto her back.

4. As soon as the attacking player has her opponent on her back in the pin, the attacker spreads her legs wider to give herself a broader base and make it more difficult for the player on the bottom to do a bridge-and-roll escape out of the pin.

COACHING TIP:
CAPITALIZE ON BASIC MISTAKES

Why are we showing you a really basic move that is usually only done by inexperienced players? Isn't this technique just using your strength? Aren't there far better ways to attempt a pin in mat work than grabbing the other player around the neck? Yes and yes. We want you to try it anyway for a couple of reasons.

First, everyone starts out as a beginner. If you are competing in the novice division in judo or grappling or are just beginning at the amateur level in mixed martial arts, a simple technique like this often works. If you are strong and can use your strength to muscle over another player at the beginning level and win, go ahead and do it. As for there being something wrong with using your strength, get over that idea right now. Telling a competitor not to use strength is like telling a basketball player not to use height. Of course if all you have is strength, you're not going to get very far.

Second, whether it is judo, grappling or MMA, when you are fighting at a lower level, people will make these basic beginner mistakes. Capitalize on them and you'll be winning on the ground from the very beginning.

SECRET NO. 2—Plan B: Counter to Head and Arm Throw to a Pin

1. The next step is to practice countering the simple throw to a pin. As Crystal Butts grabs around Ronda Rousey's neck, Rousey grabs the sleeve at the elbow. (See arrow.) At the same time, she grabs Butts around the waist, her hand going under the opponent's left arm—as the opponent grabs high, Rousey goes for the waist.

2. Rousey swings her hips in front of her opponent. (Often, the students we teach will compare this to hula dancing.) Butts is trying to get her hips in front, but Rousey grabs around the waist and gets her hips in front instead. Notice that Rousey is pulling with her right hand. She is going to turn and throw her opponent onto her back.

3. Rousey continues pulling with her right hand and turning until her opponent is on her back. Rousey's left arm is behind her opponent's back and she is on top of it. It is key that she does not pull her left hand out.

4. Again, once Rousey has the pin, she spreads her legs to give herself a broader base and make it harder for the opponent to lift her and roll her over her body.

COACHING TIP: PRACTICE TO PERFECTION

After you have a pin, get a *better* pin. As Vince Lombardi said, "Practice doesn't make perfect. Perfect practice makes perfect."

However you say it, the point is that you want to practice every drill, every repetition, doing it as close to perfect as you possibly can. The difference between being No. 1 in the world and No. 100 isn't so much the hours on the mat. It's what you are doing in those hours.

SECRET NO. 2—Plan C: Inside-Turn Escape

Crystal Butts is going to do an inside-turn escape. Ronda Rousey has her arm under the right side of Butts' body. Notice that when Butts does the escape, she turns to her left. Her right arm is going inside between her body and Rousey's. That is how this escape got the name "inside turn." The escaping player continues to pull her left arm away, turns in toward her opponent, gets up on her knees and gets out of the pin.

SECRET NO. 2—Plan D: Four-Corner Hold Counter to Inside-Turn Escape

1. The final move in this sequence is a reaction to an opponent's attempted escape. As Crystal Butts does the inside turn, Ronda Rousey uses her right arm to hook her opponent's right arm.

2. She then takes a big step with her back leg (the right, in this instance) around toward the opponent's head.

3. Rousey continues to drive her bodyweight behind the arm hooking Butts' arm until Rousey is lying facedown, pinning her opponent. Also, notice that Rousey is up on her toes—she is putting all her weight on Butts' head. Not a comfortable position for the opponent.

SECRET NO. 3

LEARN A HALF NELSON

Learn a half nelson, and if you already know it, use it. Often, no one will use this basic move during an entire tournament. The odd thing is, plenty of men, and a few women, who wrestled in high school and won many matches seem to forget all the mat work they know when they get on the judo mat or in the cage. And many people in judo, mixed martial arts and jiu-jitsu don't even know what a half nelson is.

Because the half nelson is an important move in your arsenal, it is covered in detail in Chapter 3 on mat-work basics. But here it is in simplest terms.

SECRET NO. 3: Half Nelson

1. Ronda Rousey starts out on the mat at the side of Travis McLaughlin and begins turning him from his stomach to his side. A perfect opening for this move is when the opponent has been knocked to the ground and is just starting to get up. She can take advantage of an opening, or she can make one. If she is on the left side, she'll slide her left hand under the opponent's left shoulder and up on his neck.

2. If he's flat on his stomach when she starts the half nelson, she can anticipate that he may get up on all fours. Notice that Rousey has her right hand ready to drive through underneath McLaughlin's body.

3. As soon as he starts to rise, she reaches for the far elbow with her right hand, pulls the elbow through and continues the half nelson.

4. Rousey follows through into a pin by pulling McLaughlin's elbow and head.

5. Notice that at the finish of the pin, Rousey has her left arm wrapped around her opponent's head. In mixed martial arts, she would be able to start punching him from this position before switching to a mount.

Alternate Ending In judo or grappling, she could continue driving with her body until the opponent is flat on his back for a pin.

SECRET NO. 4

PERFECT PRACTICE MAKES PERFECT

So far, we've talked about what to do. Equally important is how you do it—train hard and smart. Not taking advantage of transition to mat work and mat-work combinations are basic mistakes people make in the strategies they use. Not doing an armbar properly and not doing a half nelson are basic mistakes in the techniques people use. Here are steps to avoiding common mistakes in training.

Even though the sequence below was taken during a speed drill, in Step 2, Rousey has one of McLaughlin's arms in both of hers, her leg pushes down and she pulls up with both hands. That's a submission. Coaches and athletes want to make sure that every repetition is done correctly. During a drill, the goal isn't to do as many techniques as possible badly in a short period, but sometimes athletes act that way. They want to get their drills over with, so they whip off 50 halfhearted techniques and are ready to jump into free practice.

SECRET NO. 4: Perfect Practice

1. Ronda Rousey is originally somewhat curled up as her right leg is bent, with her foot above Travis McLaughlin's left knee.

2. Notice how tight she is to her opponent's shoulder. As she stretches out everything—her leg, her body—his arm goes straight.

SECRET NO. 5

PRACTICE EVERY TECHNIQUE RIGHT AND LEFT

Let us emphasize again: Do the same technique on the right and left sides. If you happen to be fighting an opponent from the side opposite the one you prefer, it is, of course, not a good idea to get up and try to switch to the other side.

We said this before and we're saying it again because we know that much of coaching is repetition. We tell a player to lock the arm against his body, but in free practice, he forgets. So we remind him. Too many times, we've had players tell us they were done with mat-work repetitions, yet when we asked whether they did both sides, they would go off grumbling to do the other half of the exercise.

SECRET NO. 5: Bilateral Practice

Here is the technique presented in Secret No. 4 but executed to the opposite side.

SECRET NO. 6

DEVELOP "SPIDER SENSE" (THE SUPER SECRET)

In the old comic books, when Spider-Man was in danger, he would say: "My spider sense is tingling." No, this isn't the part of the book when we tell you how to develop superpowers. Sorry. You should, though, be able to sense when you are in danger on that mat. One dangerous position is when you are trying to do mat work from between the legs, what jiu-jitsu players refer to as "in the guard." This isn't a good attacking position. You need to either split the legs—that is, get one leg up pinned down to the mat—or get around the person's legs completely. The second dangerous position is when you are on the bottom defending. If you stay on the mat in a defensive position long enough, you're going to lose. Average players, when they find themselves on the bottom in mat work, get the hell out of there.

Being on the bottom is not always a bad thing, though. There are several attacks from there—a wrestler's roll, for example, or a sit-out to an armbar. Really skilled mat technicians attack when they find themselves on the bottom. Sometimes they are even deliberately on the bottom to lure the opponent into engaging in mat work. If you are attacking, the opponent has to spend at least 50 percent of his or her attention on defending and only has 50 percent attention left to attack.

Those players who attack from the bottom are the exception, though. Most players who stay on the bottom do so because they don't have any way of getting out and are hoping the referee will save them. No one ever won a match by defending. We've heard all the excuses, too, so don't try arguing with us by saying, "I was trying to attack from there." Unless you won the match, you weren't attacking very successfully, now, were you?

If you are repeatedly in one of these "dangerous" positions, that shows a lack of mat-work "sense." If you can't sense when you're in a position that's to your disadvantage and you can't come up with a way to get out of it, you need to spend a lot more time during free practice on ground work and mat-work drills.

SECRET NO. 6: Develop "Spider Sense"

Really skilled mat technicians attack when they find themselves on the bottom. Players who attack from the bottom, though, are the exception.

THIS IS A TEST

Before going on to the rest of the book, write down one technique for each of these situations that you perform well enough to do in competition. That is, note techniques that you can make work against an opponent who is resisting you, not just those that you can do in a demonstration.

You're knocked down with your back to the ground and the opponent is standing in front of you.	
You've knocked down your opponent, his/her back is to the mat and you are standing in front.	
You miss a technique or are pulled down so that you are on your hands and knees and your opponent is standing in front of you.	
Your opponent misses a technique or is pulled down so that he/she is on his/her hands and knees in front of you.	
You miss a technique or are pulled down so that you are in front of your opponent with one knee on the ground and still holding on.	
Your opponent misses a technique or is pulled down so that he/she is in front of you with one knee on the ground and still holding on.	
You are on all fours with the opponent at your side.	
The opponent is on all fours with you at the side.	
You are on your back. The opponent is between your legs.	
Your opponent is on his/her back. You're between his/her legs.	
You have been thrown to your stomach and your opponent is behind you.	
Your opponent has been thrown to the stomach and you are behind him/her.	

How Did You Do on the Test?

Were there positions from which you could not think of an attack you could do? Have you actually *won* matches with all the techniques you listed, or are you just telling yourself, "Sure, I do that well enough to win with it in competition."

There should be no position, no place on the mat, where your opponent is safe from you. In fact, you should have at least two techniques for each position in case the first one doesn't work. Follow the advice in this book and you'll pass that test with flying colors.

CHAPTER 2:

MAT-WORK CONNECTIONS: A DOZEN QUICK WAYS TO A SUBMISSION

Our theory of mat work can be summed up as the following: "Everything connects to something else." These four points explain it in a little more detail.

1. Begin with a few basic techniques as building blocks.

2. Connect these building blocks together to make a series.

3. Connect these series together.

4. Drill these series until you react automatically and you will always be half a step ahead of your opponent.

One difference in the way we teach mat work is in our emphasis on combinations. You are going to be a lot better at ground work if you have mat techniques that fit together. When adding a new mat technique to your arsenal, try to think about how it fits with what you already have. Our first example of mat techniques that fit together starts with an attempted throw by the opponent. From this position, you go to an armbar. If that doesn't work, move to a second armbar. If that fails, move to a third armbar.

NO. 1: ARMBAR SUBMISSION AS A COUNTER TO A THROW (TOMOE NAGE ARMBAR)

We like this transition because it is often unexpected. This technique begins with a common situation in a match—one person gets knocked down, either for a score or a slight advantage. You practice this technique starting from a standing position, the opponent knocks you on your butt or side and attacks trying to follow up an advantage. We call it the *tomoe nage* armbar because the beginning of it looks similar to the judo throw of the same name.

NO. 1: Armbar Submission as a Counter to a Throw (Tomoe Nage Armbar)

1. Ronda Rousey starts with a standard grip: right hand on the lapel and left hand on the judo gi. (If the opponent is not wearing a gi, grab the back of his or her neck and wrist.)

2. Travis McLaughlin gets a grip and tries to throw or push her backward. If she feels herself losing her balance and falling to her back, she'll place her right foot above his knee and push.

3. The second she touches the ground, as he stretches out, she lets go of the lapel grip she had with her right hand and grabs his wrist. Now she has two hands on one arm. At the same time, she'll throw her left leg over his arm. Notice how close Rousey is to McLaughlin. This is a really important point: Giving him too much space allows him to block the armbar and pin her. (If this happens to you the next time you try it, step with your left foot in closer to your opponent.)

4. Rousey pushes his leg away with the foot she has placed above his knee. This should cause him to stretch his arm out and fall forward. She locks the arm tight to her body and arches her hips to complete the armbar.

5. If McLaughlin manages to pull away and starts to stand up, she can lock his arm tight against her body and arch her hips for the armbar.

NO. 2: TOMOE NAGE ARMBAR WITH ARMBAR ESCAPE ATTEMPT

What if the first armbar attempt doesn't work? In the photos for the armbar submission as a counter to a throw, if the player did not manage to get her foot above the opponent's knee and push his leg out, he could have tried a forward roll to escape. Here's an alternative plan.

NO. 2: Tomoe Nage Armbar With Armbar Escape Attempt

1. Like in the No. 1 combination, Ronda Rousey has a right standard grip: right hand on the lapel and left hand on the sleeve.

2. Again, she puts her right foot on Travis McLaughlin's left leg above the knee.

3. Rousey lets go of the lapel with her right hand and grabs the sleeve (or the wrist). She prefers to grab the sleeve when doing judo, as shown; she grabs the wrist in MMA competition. Some judo players grab the wrist in judo competition, as well. It is completely a matter of personal preference.

4. Rousey pushes with her foot placed above McLaughlin's knee. As his leg gets pushed away from her, his arm will be straightened out.

5. To escape the armbar, he may try to roll his arm so that instead of his elbow being to the side, it is now pointing up toward the ceiling. He has twisted out of the armbar.

6. She keeps hold of his arm and turns with him. Refer back to Step 4. Notice that she was on her side and his elbow was turned to the side. When he turned so he was facedown and his elbow was toward the ceiling, she turned with him. His elbow remained locked against her body.

7. If she can stop his roll right here, she'll lock his arm to her body and do a one-handed push-up from the floor. This puts her pelvis directly on his elbow. Again, she arches her hips to complete the armbar.

NO. 3: ARMBAR COUNTER TO A THROW WITH TWO ESCAPE ATTEMPTS

The secret to success with an armbar submission—or with any mat work, in fact—is to be one step ahead of your opponent. We'll make this comment many times in this book because it is a key point we want you to remember. This next move starts like the two previous ones, but this one includes two escape attempts.

Briefly, you start from a standing position and go to one armbar, with your opponent's arm locked against your body. If he twists onto his stomach, lock his arm against your body and push up, trying a second armbar. If he tries a forward roll, follow him, locking the arm against your body and arching, doing a third armbar.

Although we did not emphasize it here (but we will in a later chapter), this drill is also good practice for the opponent in trying to get out of armbars. We know very few people who practice armbar escapes. Perhaps that is why so few people get out of armbars.

NO. 3: Armbar Counter to a Throw With Two Escape Attempts

1. As before, Ronda Rousey begins with a right standard grip, with her right hand on Travis McLaughlin's lapel and her left hand on the sleeve.

2. Again, she puts her right foot on his left leg above the knee.

3. She lets go of the lapel with the right hand and grabs the sleeve (or the wrist). Rousey grabs the sleeve when doing judo and the wrist in MMA competitions. Some judo players grab the wrist in judo competitions, as well.

4. She pushes with her foot placed above his knee. As his leg gets pushed away from her, his arm will be straightened out.

5. To escape the armbar, the opponent may try to roll his arm so that instead of his elbow being to the side, it is now pointing up toward the ceiling. He has twisted out of the armbar.

6. She keeps hold of his arm and turns with him. Refer to Step 4. Notice that Rousey was on her side and McLaughlin's elbow was turned to the side. When he turned, she turned with him and now she is facedown, still with his arm tight against her body.

Continued on next page

7. This time, though, he is a little faster and a little shrewder than in the tomoe nage armbar with an armbar escape attempt. He continues turning his trapped arm and pushes up from the mat with his free arm.

8. McLaughlin does a forward roll in an attempt to escape the armbar.

9. Rousey follows him over, with the arm still locked against her body, and once again, she arches her hips to apply the armbar. A side note on perfect technique: Rousey has her knees tight together. She has both hands at her opponent's wrist, locking the forearm against her body, her legs are squeezed together holding him tight at the shoulder, her knees are tight, allowing no space for him to pull his arm through (if he did, by some miracle, manage to pull his wrist free), and her legs are bent, curling his body back toward her with her feet. (A leg curl done at the gym is the same motion.)

NO. 4: ROLLOVER FROM THE GUARD TO PIN TO BENT-ARM-LOCK COMBINATION

Another type of connection starts from a base and branches out. A few notes about this combination: By Step 6, notice that the player still has her opponent's arm trapped and still has the same grip on his head that she had when this sequence began. Also at that point, she has a pin that will win a match in judo or earn points in a grappling tournament. She also has a choke, squeezing her opponent's neck and putting all her weight on it. It's possible, though, that a particularly tough opponent will resist and not give up. To be honest, it's not a particularly great choke, but the choke is not what she's really going for here.

NO. 4: Rollover From the Guard to Pin to Bent-Arm-Lock Combination

1. The base begins with Ronda Rousey sitting up and the opponent in front of her.

2. She hooks over Travis McLaughlin's arm above the elbow and grabs his head.

3. She leans back, pulling him up on his knees and toward her. Her right leg is on the outside of her opponent's body and her left leg is going to hook on the inside of his right leg.

4. She rolls to her side and makes a scissors motion with her legs as she does. The outside leg (the one that is overhooking) is turning in, and the inside leg is underhooking, lifting him up, in order to turn him over.

Continued on next page

5. As McLaughlin rolls onto his back, Rousey lifts her hips.

6. She steps her left leg in front, driving her weight on to her opponent's head, pushing off with her right leg.

7. Rousey sinks her hips down, lowering her center of gravity and spreading her legs wide. Whether it's judo or no-gi grappling, this is still a pin and she is still scoring points.

8. If she loosens up just a little with her arm, the opponent will pull away, thinking he has a chance to escape.

9. She catches his bent arm at the wrist and pushes it down. She lifts the leg that is closest to his head and hooks his arm with it.

10. Rousey pushes forward with her hips while applying pressure downward with her leg until he taps.

11. To make this a tighter armbar, she hooks her foot under her own knee to make a figure-4 on the arm, then arches forward with her hips while applying pressure downward with the leg that has his arm hooked. His wrist is pinned to the mat while his elbow is pushed upward.

NO. 5: ROLLOVER FROM THE GUARD TO MOUNT TO ARM-LOCK COMBINATION

This "collect the arm" move is a basis for a lot of possibilities. The pin to the bent-arm lock previously discussed is one. A second possibility from this same move is to roll up on top for what judo players call the upper four-corner hold down *(tate shiho gatame),* and Brazilian *jiu-jitsu* players call it the mount.

A few notes about this move: First, although we break it down into steps, it takes less than 30 seconds from start to finish. In fact, Rousey won one of her MMA matches with this armbar in 25 seconds, from the time it took to clinch up, take the opponent down and apply the armbar. Second, in the last step, she has actually loosened up on the armbar a bit and is looking at her partner as he is tapping. This is a good example of taking care of your teammates. If you are practicing armbars, you want to look out for your partner. In judo, we call this the principle of mutual benefit and welfare. Or you could call it, "If you act like too much of a jerk, no one will practice with you."

NO. 5: Rollover From the Guard to Mount to Arm-Lock Combination

1. The starting position is the same as in the pin to the bent-arm lock.

2. Collect the arm: Ronda Rousey hooks above Travis McLaughlin's elbow and takes a grip on the opposite side of his shirt. Rousey traps his arm, and she keeps this grip through the whole move and never lets it go.

3a. She rolls him, sweeping with the outside leg and lifting with the inside leg. As before, she over-hooks the opponent's arm above the elbow.

3b. At the same time, her inside leg hooks his leg and lifts, and her arm goes around his head as she rolls.

4. She rolls over all the way on top of the opponent. Now she has several options. In judo or grappling, this is a pin. She can stay in this position for points or move to a submission.

Continued on next page

5. Mixed martial arts allows the option of coming up into a striking position. If her opponent tries to turn to his stomach to escape, he is very likely to turn in the direction where her fist is up because there is a large opening there. In this case, it is to his right.

6. Not coincidentally, when McLaughlin turns, Rousey's right arm is in the exact position to hook over his arm.

7. As he turns, she rolls with him, locking her body tight to his arm. (When Rousey does this move, she puts her other hand—the one not gripping the arm—out in front of her to put all her weight on the opponent and stabilize her balance. Another option is to have both arms locked on the opponent's arm from the very beginning. Try it both ways to see which one works for you.)

8. Rousey steps over McLaughlin's body with her right leg, still keeping his left arm trapped tight against her body with her right arm. Her hips are tight against her opponent's body.

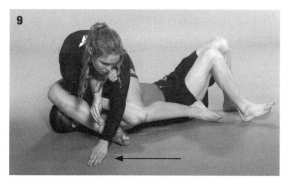

9. As Rousey leans backward, her left hand comes off the mat to catch McLaughlin's left arm.

10. Leaning back, Rousey's legs come together. She pinches her knees tight to hold the left arm and to prevent him from reaching up and grabbing with his opposite arm to try to defend.

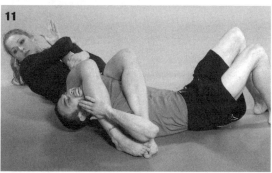

11. Holding the arm tight against her body with both hands, she thrusts upward with her pelvis to apply the armbar.

HOW THE
COLLECT-THE-ARM DRILL GOT ITS NAME

When famed mixed-martial artist Gokor Chivichyan first came to the United States, he was asked by one of the local judo clubs to teach mat work. New to the English language, he began his explanation by saying, "First, you collect the arm. ..." Everyone laughed, but later on, instructors found that the expression really captured the attention of their young students and helped them remember the technique. The name stuck.

NO. 6: VARIATION ON THE MOUNT TO ARM-LOCK COMBINATION

This is very similar to technique No. 5. Any time we do a clinic or teach a class, there is always that one student who asks, "But what if they don't try to escape? What if they don't turn in that direction?" Well, then you do this variation.

NO. 6: Variation on the Mount to Arm-Lock Combination

1. Ronda Rousey collects the arm by overhooking Crystal Butts' left arm above the elbow with her right arm. At the same time, she hooks her left leg inside the opponent's right thigh.

2. Her next step is to roll hard toward the opponent's left side, sweeping with her right leg and lifting with her left. Notice that Rousey has her leg hooked inside and is using her whole body to roll her opponent. She is rolling toward the same side where she has the arm "collected" so that the opponent doesn't have that arm free to post out. When doing this move, if Rousey swings her arm as she goes over and basically hits the opponent in the side of the neck with her biceps, it adds to the momentum. This is legal in judo and grappling because it does not count as a strike.

3. She continues the scissoring motion of sweeping with her right leg and lifting with her left until her opponent is on her back.

4. She rolls all the way on top of Butts into the pin. If this was a judo competition, she could stay here for 25 seconds to win the match. In grappling, she would gain points.

5. In mixed martial arts, she could come up at this point and begin striking her opponent.

6. Rather than turning to her side, Butts puts up her left arm to defend. Rousey grabs the wrist with her left hand, pulling the arm away from her opponent's body. She overhooks the opponent's arm with her right arm, making sure she is above the elbow.

7. Rousey leans forward to lock her body against her opponent's arm.

Continued on next page

8. She steps over with her right leg. With the opponent's arm locked against her body with her right arm, she can put her left hand out to help balance as she steps over. The opponent may now try to turn to escape the armbar, but it is too late.

9. As she leans backward, Rousey pulls the arm toward her opponent's head as if to rip the arm out. The left hand comes back and traps the opponent's forearm, so now she has two hands on her one. At the same time, Rousey's legs are squeezing together. When she is pulling her adversary's arms apart, she applies pressure at the wrist to separate the arms because this is a much weaker point and more effective than pulling at the elbow or upper arm.

10. With her back to the mat, Rousey arches with her hips to apply the armbar.

NO. 7: ROLLOVER FROM GUARD TO PIN/CHOKE TO ARM-LOCK COMBINATION

This technique starts in a fashion similar to the prior ones, but it involves pinning from the side instead of from the top. It seems to have become popular to call someone who repeatedly wins by the same technique, such as an armbar, "a one-trick pony." That "one trick" has many possible entries into it. It's not one trick; it is several different tricks.

Briefly, you can start from standing and go to an armbar, then use a combination if that first armbar attempt does not work, then another combination if the second attempt is blocked. Next, you "collect the arm" and use several different possibilities from there. You can roll on top into the mount and begin striking, then catch the straight-arm lock as your opponent tries to turn. You can get the same armbar from the same position if your opponent does not try to roll away but simply puts up an arm to block. You can do one of a couple of different pins, either from the top or side, combined with a choke. When your opponent attempts to escape from the pin, you can apply either a bent-arm lock or a straight-arm lock, depending on which way the opponent tries to escape.

By now, you should see why it is not so easy to defend against someone whose "only trick is an armbar." First, there is not just *one* armbar. Second, there are many ways of getting into that one armbar. Sometimes, your opponent's choice is being choked, staying on the ground being punched in the face or giving up an arm for that armbar.

In the following sequence, note that people who are not very tough can be convinced to tap out on the pin in Step 8 because it hurts, especially if the player is in the position with her feet up by the opponent's hips and putting all her weight on her face. This isn't a really effective choke as far as cutting off the blood supply to the brain and making the opponent go unconscious, but it hurts, so some people will tap.

NO. 7: Rollover From Guard to Pin/Choke to Arm-Lock Combination

1. As before, Ronda Rousey hooks over her opponent's arm above the elbow and has her leg on the outside of the side where the arm is "collected." In this case, Rousey has Crystal Butts' left arm hooked with her right arm and has her right leg on the outside.

2. Again, she rolls to the side where she has the arm trapped (in this case, it is her opponent's left side), which would be to her right. She sweeps with her outside leg.

3. With the other leg, she hooks on the inside of her opponent's opposite leg and lifts.

4. She goes all the way over to the opponent's side into the pin.

5. In judo, this can win the match. Rousey keeps the arm locked exactly as she has from Step 1. She spreads her legs as shown, with one knee up and putting her weight on Butts, her head locked tight.

6. Rousey baits the opponent by loosening her grip on the arm and letting her "get away."

7. Then she shoves the arm that "escaped" across her opponent's face. She clasps her hands together tightly and squeezes.

8. To make this pin-and-choke combination more painful, Rousey can move her legs to use her bodyweight to put more pressure on the choke. She puts one knee into her opponent's shoulder to make the pin tighter. Driving off from her other leg, she puts all her weight on her opponent's face and neck while applying the choke. (In judo, this pin is called a kata gatame.) Many times, the opponent will tap out and this is the end.

Continued on next page

9. If the opponent does not tap out of the pin, Rousey keeps the upper body held tightly and steps over into the mount. She maintains pressure on the head to apply the choke. Note that Rousey clasps her hands tightly together to put pressure on her opponent's neck. She also stays up on her toes, putting all her weight on her opponent's head.

10. Even really tough people will be distracted when you almost dislocate their jaw, which brings their attention away from escaping the pin. What they tend to do in such situations is try to get away by pushing that arm that is shoved against their face. The opponent has two choices—either get choked or turn away to relieve the pressure from the choke. As Butts turns, Rousey steps over, hooking the arm with her right arm.

11. Rousey locks the arm tight against her body with both arms, leans back and arches.

COACHING TIP:
AVOID THESE MISTAKES

It is *good* to have a connected sequence of mat techniques. However, before leaving this topic, we want to make sure we don't leave you with any false ideas. The first mistake you should avoid is assuming that it is really hard to learn this level of mat work. Actually, it's not. You don't need to learn every single one of the steps right away. You learn one technique and then you connect it to the others.

The second mistake we don't want you to make is to assume that everything needs to be connected directly to everything else. For example, the Klaus Glahn turnover (see No. 8), named after the German Olympic medalist of the same name, is a good connection from a turnover straight into a choke and pin, but it doesn't connect to moves No. 6 and No. 7. You need to be "dangerous" to your opponent no matter what position he or she takes on the mat.

NO. 8: TURNOVER, PIN AND CHOKE (KLAUS GLAHN)

Here is how this next turnover, pin and choke "connects" to the mat work of someone who is good at armbars (as demonstrated in the first example) and who has a successful turnover when she is in the guard and her opponent attacks (as in the second example). Rather than confronting Rousey head-on, her opponent, Butts, has curled up in a defensive position, with both arms pulled in close. She is protecting her arms and not taking a chance on moving directly toward Rousey to allow her to sit back into the guard and "collect the arm." Notice that the opponent can't really protect the back of the neck from this position. If she does reach a hand up, it's just inviting an armbar.

NO. 8: Turnover, Pin and Choke (Klaus Glahn)

1. Ronda Rousey grabs Crystal Butts' gi behind the neck with her left hand, palm up, while her right hand slides across and grabs the opposite lapel. She pulls her opponent up into her. Butts is now pulled in tight toward Rousey.

Hand Position Demonstration

Butts is up on her knees to demonstrate the correct hand position in Step 1. Obviously, though, when you are doing this in practice or at a tournament, your opponent is not going to be so helpful. She will be on knees and elbows as shown in the first photo.

2. Rousey straightens out her right leg and drops her right elbow down so that she now has her opponent's neck between her wrists.

3. Rousey rolls hard to the left. Because the opponent is pulled in tight, she is going to roll with Rousey—besides, she has her neck.

4. The roll continues until she is on top of her opponent.

5a. She now has a choice. She can come up and apply the choke, holding on tightly with both hands as she pulls her elbows apart.

5b. Or as she pulls her elbows apart, Rousey can let go with the left hand and hook it under the opponent's neck. She shoves the opponent's left hand across her face, clasps her hands together and uses her head (literally) to squeeze her arm and neck even tighter. At the end, to make the pin even tighter and more uncomfortable, she hooks her legs into the opponent's at the ankles and spreads her legs apart.

NO. 9: ARM LOCK TO PIN AND BACK AGAIN

A bigger mistake than thinking everything needs to be connected is to get so focused on one move that you forget to make those connections. An error we have seen too many times in competition is when a player attempts an armbar against an opponent who is resisting very strongly, like in Step 1 in this combination. Often, nothing happens in this position. The player on the top exerts a lot of effort trying to get the armbar, but the player on the bottom has both arms locked together resisting. The referee stops the match, and both players get up. Here is what *should* happen.

NO. 9: Arm Lock to Pin and Back Again

1. Ronda Rousey attempts an armbar, and before she can get her body locked on to the opponent's arm, she pulls her elbow in tight and grabs her hand, wrist or judo gi with the other hand. If she slides her other arm through, she is in a battle of strength, pulling against the opponent's two arms with hers.

2. Instead, using the hand nearest the opponent's hips (here, that's Rousey's right hand), she feeds the bottom of the opponent's jacket into her other hand. Notice here that Rousey is feeding the gi into her hand over her leg.

3. She grabs Crystal Butts' far leg.

4. Rousey swings that leg toward her, keeping her ankles locked together. She does a leg curl to pull Butts tight to her. Pulling in tight with both legs and with her ankles crossed allows no space for the opponent to turn away. She also still has that arm trapped with her arm threaded through it and holding the opponent's jacket in her hand. Of course, if Butts lets go, Rousey is going to lean back and armbar her.

5. Rousey puts her free hand on the mat to block her opponent from turning away to escape the pin.

6a. She moves her leg from across the opponent's face to behind her and sits up on the opponent for the pin. She can stay here and win the match.

6b. Or if Butts lets go of her own hand and tries to escape the pin, Rousey immediately gets up on her back leg, leaning her bodyweight on the opponent's arm.

Continued on next page

7. Now she throws her back leg across her opponent's face, keeping the arm locked tight to her body.

8. She leans back and arches her hips for the armbar. In this position, Rousey still has her right arm across her opponent. Another option is to hold the opponent's arm with both her arms.

NO. 10: ARM LOCK TO PIN AND BACK AGAIN—PLAN B

This next arm lock is similar to No. 9. The situation starts the same, with the opponent defending against an attempt at an armbar. The pin is done differently, and here is why. In No. 9, Rousey was really trying to pin her opponent, going through several steps to get a tight pin. If the pin had failed and Butts started to escape, Rousey would have gone back to the armbar. An alternative scenario, plan B, is a little different. Here, the player isn't really trying to pin the opponent. The goal is to get her to let go of that arm so she can armbar her.

Note that after Step 4 in this sequence, the player can do one of two things. Although it may seem strange to step over, grab the arm and lean back for the armbar (when it would be more efficient just to do the push-up armbar shown in 5a), in fact, the second armbar tends to be tighter. In our experience, the second armbar (5b) is harder to escape.

NO. 10: Arm Lock to Pin and Back Again—Plan B

1. Ronda Rousey has Crystal Butts' arm hooked, but she has clasped her hands together, so now it is two arms against two arms. The strongest person will win in this situation. In judo, the referee will stand them both up after a few seconds in this position.

2. Rousey steps a leg across her opponent's face back behind her. She hooks her other leg under the opponent's shoulder, locking the opponent's arm against her body by sitting up close to it, putting all her weight on her opponent's upper body.

3. It really does not matter where Rousey's right hand is. Here, she has it near Butts' hips, in part to make the pin a little more secure but mostly to make the opponent think she is really trying to pin.

Continued on next page

4. Sensing that it is easy to get out of this pin, Butts lets go of her own hand and turns to her side to escape.

5a. Rousey can lock the arm straight against her body by pushing up with the right arm and arching her hips forward to apply the armbar.

5b. Or she can catch the opponent's wrist with her right hand. She now has the opponent's arm locked straight against her body with both her arms. Instead of two arms against two arms, like in Step 1, she has her two arms against the opponent's one arm, which gives her much better odds. All she needs to do is lean back and thrust upward with her hips to apply the armbar.

NO. 11: SHOULDER THROW TO ARM LOCK

The transition between standing and ground work is one of the most often missed opportunities to win a match. This example begins with a one-arm shoulder throw *(ippon seoi nage,* in judo terms) into an arm lock. Notice that Rousey is doing the throw to the left side.

In Step 6 of this sequence, some people might prefer to keep the right foot, the one near the opponent's head, in place instead of to the left. Either way is fine—do whatever works for you. Keeping one foot planted prevents the opponent from turning in to escape the armbar. Another way to do this move is to jump up in the air with both feet off the ground and land on your back, like in a backward breakfall, and throw both legs across the opponent's body at once. Given the element of surprise, this very often works, especially if you have practiced the technique enough so that there is no hesitation between the throw and arm lock. The jumping-in-the-air armbar looks impressive, but it is not as secure as the first method. It is just showing off.

NO. 11: Shoulder Throw to Arm Lock

1. Ronda Rousey starts with a standard grip, one hand on Travis McLaughlin's lapel and one on his sleeve at the elbow.

2. She lets go of the lapel, grabs above the opponent's elbow and turns into the throw.

Continued on next page

3. Bending at the knees, she continues turning so that her opponent rolls off her shoulder.

4. She throws the opponent over her shoulder onto the mat. Note that this is not a perfect judo throw and will not earn a high score in a judo match.

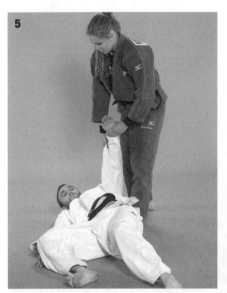

5. When she throws the opponent, he'll land in front of her on his side. Her right leg is near his head, keeping him from turning toward her to escape. She is still holding his arm at the elbow, and his arm is already straight, with her legs on either side of it.

6. Rousey sits down in place, without letting go of McLaughlin's arm or moving her left foot. As she sits, she throws her right leg over his body and slides both her hands up to his wrist.

7. She locks his arm against her body and arches with her hips to apply pressure to the elbow.

HOW DESTROYING MY KNEE MADE ME A WORLD CHAMPION

At a young age, I had what should have been a career-ending injury. My knee was so damaged that it became physically impossible to balance on my right leg and throw someone—eliminating a whole range of throws. Eventually, my other knee started to give out from years of bearing 80 percent of my weight, and it became increasingly difficult for me to lift anyone even when standing on both legs. The reasonable decision was to quit competing. Instead, I set a goal of winning the World Judo Championships. Because I couldn't throw very well, my only winning option was to follow up from those less-than-perfect throws and win on the mat.

—*AnnMaria De Mars*

NO. 12: HEEL HOOK TO MOUNT TO ARM LOCK

How is it possible that a few competitors like Ronda Rousey, AnnMaria De Mars and Jimmy Pedro Jr. manage to win with the same arm lock over and over? Wouldn't people see it coming? Certainly, at least some of their opponents expected those exact moves and trained to defend against them. So what happened?

One answer is that when a person is thrown, he or she often hesitates for a fraction of a second, as if in shock that the opponent managed the knockdown. This hesitation is your opportunity to move into mat work and set up the arm lock while your opponent is focused on defending against something else. We will return to this point again and again throughout the book.

The throw to arm-lock combination (No. 11) is one example—the opponent was focused on turning out of the throw and not thinking about the arm lock. Here is a second example. Note that Rousey is doing the technique left-handed. To do it right-handed, she would simply reverse the grip and hook the right heel with her right foot.

NO. 12: Heel Hook to Mount to Arm Lock

1. The standard grip is one hand on the opponent's elbow and the other on his lapel. In a no-gi event, the second hand can grab the opponent's shoulder or neck instead, as shown.

2. Ronda Rousey pulls herself into Travis McLaughlin and hooks his left heel with her left foot. She sweeps the foot forward and to the opponent's right while driving her upper body into him.

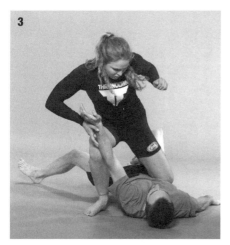

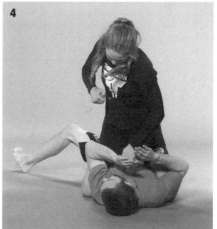

3. As she knocks her opponent down, she follows him to the mat. He feels that his arm is in danger, so he pulls it in, actually helping to pull Rousey on top of his upper body.

4. She pulls her legs up into the mount and starts striking. (In judo, she can apply an upper four-corner hold.)

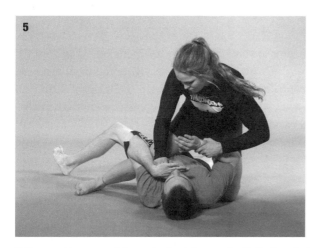

5. Because the opponent does not enjoy being punched in the face, he is going to try to put his hands up to block and turn away from her. Rousey grabs the upper hand at the wrist—in this case, he chose to put his right hand up, so she grabbed it with her left hand. Although they are not wearing judo gi and this is not a throw, this is a very judo move. Rousey is using McLaughlin's own momentum against him. As he puts his hand up to block, she catches it and uses his own motion, pulling his wrist toward her. She is never going to let go of this wrist.

Continued on next page

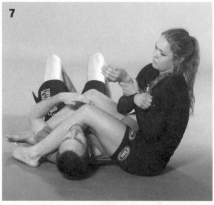

6. She leans her body forward, locking his arm against her body. She slides her right arm between their bodies, catching his arm at the forearm. Now both her arms are locking his forearm against her chest.

7. Rousey steps over with her back leg so that she has both legs across McLaughlin's body. She curls his body toward her, as if doing a leg curl. She locks the arm against her body. She leans back and arches up with her hips to execute the armbar.

LESSON LEARNED

We hope as you read through this chapter that you found yourself thinking, "Hey, didn't I just read that technique a few pages back?" or "I could do the second technique with this one." Exactly. You can take these dozen quick ways to a submission and combine them in 30 or 40 different ways. You may have observed that many of the techniques ended in the same armbar, mount or pin and that it is easy to go back and forth between those positions. A key feature you'll notice about our mat work is that it is connected and it is because of these connections that your opponent is left with literally nowhere to turn. Every direction that opponent moves, you have another technique waiting. This is the secret to being dangerous on the mat. There should be no move your opponents can make that will keep him or her safe from you.

CHAPTER 3

TWO MAT-WORK TECHNIQUES EVERYONE SHOULD KNOW

Have you ever watched a competition and seen a dozen missed opportunities for winning on the ground? Whether it's grappling, judo or mixed martial arts, a match starts with the players standing, one person tries a technique, they hit the mat and then—nothing. They seem to flail around for a while, maybe one or both of them attempts a mat-work move, there is no real progress and the referee restarts the match with both competitors standing. This not only is boring for the spectators but also is a lost opportunity for one of the players to win. If an opponent is on his back, it's a chance to do an armbar. If he is on his stomach, it's a chance to do a half nelson to put him on his back and then maybe do an armbar. We briefly discussed half nelsons and armbars in the previous chapter. We're going to go into a little more detail here because if you don't have both these basic techniques down cold, there is a gaping hole in your ground game.

HOW TO DO A PERFECT ARMBAR

There are a few basic points you need to know to do an armbar right. When you do an armbar, lock the opponent's arm against your body. You should not be using your arms trying to pull the person's arm in any direction. The most efficient way to do an armbar is to hold the opponent's arm tight against your body, between your legs.

If the opponent is on his back with his hands clasped together, lock the arm against your chest and rotate toward his head. Lock his arm against your chest with both your arms and pull to the left, not straight backward. Once you have ripped his arm loose from the other hand, then you can rotate back at a right angle to his body. Whenever you are in this position, arch your hips upward to finish the armbar. Don't worry about perfection during competition. If you win, it may not have been perfect, but it was good enough.

In brief, here are the important armbar points to remember:

- Lock the arm against your body.
- Rotate toward the head to break the arm free.
- When you have the arm free, rotate back again.

ARMBAR POINTS TO REMEMBER

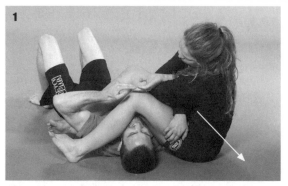

1. Ronda Rousey locks Travis McLaughlin's arm against her body and is pulling to her left. (See the direction of the arrow.)

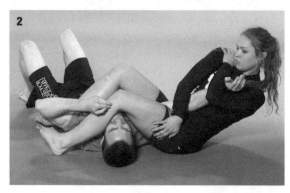

2. She rotates toward his head to break the arm free. When she has the arm free, she rotates back again.

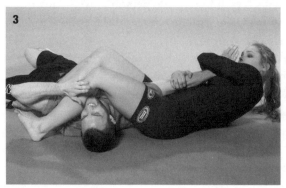

3. Rousey locks his arm against her body. She has perfect form on her upper body because she has no space between her body and McLaughlin's arm. This is precisely the way to do an armbar in judo, too, but we deliberately show it without the judo gi so that it is obvious how tight the arm is against her body. Rousey's legs are a little too far apart for this to be a perfect armbar. However, she has the arm so tight to her upper body that she is almost certain to get the submission anyway.

HOW TO DO A PERFECT ARMBAR

1. Crystal Butts is lying on her back, holding on to her own arm with all her strength to try to stop the armbar. Ronda Rousey slides the arm nearest Butts' head underneath to hold her arm tight. Rousey puts one hand up on her own shoulder and crosses the other arm over. Now she is holding the opponent's arm to herself with both her arms. She uses her ankles to pull Butts in close.

2. Rousey rotates hard toward the opponent's head, keeping the arm tight.

3. Once she rips the arm free, she rotates back into position to be at a right angle to the opponent.

4. During the entire armbar, Rousey never allows any space between her body and the opponent's. She never lets up on having her entire bodyweight pulling against the opponent's arms, and she keeps using her legs to pull the opponent tight to her throughout the entire movement.

Leg Position

Some people like to scissor their ankles and pull the opponent in. Other people like to pinch their knees together, curling the opponent in, as world judo champion and 2012 Olympic gold-medalist Kayla Harrison is doing against Aaron Kunihiro. Both methods work perfectly fine. If you win, it's right.

HOW NOT TO DO AN ARMBAR

The attacker—Crystal Butts—does not have the correct position for an armbar. There is a lot of space between her chest and Ronda Rousey's arm. In every successful armbar, there is no space between the attacker and the opponent's arm.

A second mistake in this armbar is that Butts' legs are not keeping Rousey from escaping. She is not using them to curl Rousey's body toward her, and her knees are spread apart. Rousey has space to drive both her arms toward the attacker, turn her shoulder and drive her elbow toward the mat to escape being armbarred.

A lot of armbars fail when space is allowed for the opponent to get away. Think about it. You're trying to force the person to submit. At this point, your opponent is very motivated to escape, and your job is not to allow even the smallest room for that escape to happen.

HOW TO DO A HALF NELSON

A half nelson is one of the most basic mat-work moves, yet many martial artists, particularly judo players, don't use it. In our view, that's a big mistake. It's a basic move for two reasons. First, situations in which you can use it occur often in a match; that is, the opponent is on his or her stomach with you on top. Second, it is a base from which a lot of other moves can start.

THE HALF NELSON

1. Janine Nakao, the player on top, begins from the opponent's side. She is up on her toes putting all her weight on Aaron Kunihiro. (In any position, the more uncomfortable you can make your opponent the more likely he or she is to make a mistake.) Nakao grabs Kunihiro's wrist and tries to pull it in toward her stomach.

2. Usually, an opponent will react by pulling the wrist out, as Kunihiro has done. Nakao's hand on the same side (the left hand if she's on the opponent's left side) is going to slide under her Kunihiro's arm. At the same time, she has her other hand near the opponent's opposite elbow so she can shove that arm forward if he tries to post with it to stop the move.

3. Nakao uses her weight to drive her arm forward under Kunihiro's arm and grab the back of his head, turning it in her direction.

4. As she starts to walk around, her hand comes back to the near side of her opponent.

Continued on next page

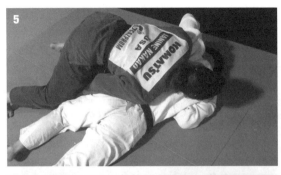

5. She slides her arm up under Kunihiro's shoulder, placing her hand on his head.

6. Nakao grabs the bottom of the jacket and continues to walk in a circle around toward the opponent's head. As his upper body starts to turn toward his back from the pressure on his neck, she uses her other hand to push his lower body over to his back, as well.

7. When he turns onto his back, she grabs under his judo gi with her right hand for a better grip in the pin and puts all her weight on his head and shoulders. Notice how Nakao, executing the pin, is up on her toes, driving all her weight onto Kunihiro's head.

THE MOST IMPORTANT BASIC MAT-WORK CONCEPT: HAVE AN ALTERNATE PLAN

Successful mat work is connected. If the opponent does not react in one way so that you can execute the first technique, have a plan B ready. This is a point we'll repeat throughout the book—connections. If you can't execute the first technique, you have a second technique to try. If that one doesn't work, you have a third technique. It's all part of your secret plan.

BASIC MAT-WORK CONCEPT: Have an Alternate Plan

1. A half nelson generally begins with one player on his or her stomach. Ronda Rousey immediately slips one hand under Manny Gamburyan's shoulder. She's going to use her right arm under his right shoulder. Note: She should have her full weight on him, as shown in the previous sequence. Here, for demonstration purposes, she is up on her knees with space between them to show her hand placement.

2. Rousey slides her right hand through to the back of his neck. Her left hand is down near his hip because she is anticipating that he will get up on his knees.

3. To keep from being turned with the half nelson, Gamburyan may try to get up on all fours, with his weight supported on his knees and far arm. (He can't use the arm near Rousey since she has leverage there because her arm is under his shoulder, grabbing the back of the head.) Here is where her plan B comes in.

4. As Gamburyan comes to his knees, Rousey puts her body-weight on him and slides her free hand underneath his body, grabs the triceps of his left arm and pulls it in.

Continued on next page

5. As Rousey drives her body-weight into Gamburyan, she slides her right hand farther on his head, pulling his arm and head toward herself and walking around his body toward his head.

6. After she has driven him onto his back into the pin, her arm should be hooked under his head as shown, with the weight of her body bearing down on his head, neck and shoulders. At this point, she'll have one hand free for striking (in mixed martial arts) or for grabbing one of his legs or another part of his body to prevent him from escaping (in judo or grappling).

CHAPTER 4

MAT-WORK SERIES: LEAVING AN OPPONENT NOWHERE TO GO

Begin with a plan in mind. The half nelson, for example, starts with an opponent flat on his stomach, and when he begins to get up, the other player is ready to reach under, grab the biceps and pull it through to complete the technique. Usually when the opponent's wrist is controlled, he or she will extend his or her arm. From that extension, the next step is to go into a half nelson, as described in the previous chapter. What if the opponent doesn't extend an arm? If the half nelson doesn't work because the opponent has pulled the arm in, then you will have wrist control.

TIE-UP SERIES

In this section, we present several more examples of mat-work connections in a series. The main consideration in doing a series of moves is anticipating your opponent's next step in case your first attempt doesn't work.

Although it may seem overwhelming initially, an important fact to keep in mind is that you don't need to learn (or teach) the whole series at once. You can work on the first technique in the series—gaining wrist control and into a pin—and once you feel comfortable with that (and once your opponents learn to expect it and escape), you can advance to the bent-arm lock. Once you have mastered the arm lock, add the choke to your repertoire.

TIE-UP SERIES: Wrist Tie-Up Turnover

1. Kayla Harrison begins by gaining wrist control, just like in the half nelson.

2. When Harrison has wrist control, Fernanda Araujo pulls her arm into her body and tries to grab her own gi or belt to give herself better positioning to counter Harrison's ability to pull her arm out.

3. Harrison keeps her body on Araujo's at all times, making her carry the weight. This should be the goal in mat work whenever one player is behind her opponent. As Harrison comes around to the front of Araujo's body (moving to her left, toward the opponent's head), her weight comes up off Araujo. The opponent usually reacts by trying to get up.

4. Coming around the front of the opponent's body, Harrison pushes Araujo's head with her knee. Harrison's elbow is in Araujo's back. Her thumb is pushing up, lifting up the opponent's elbow. Harrison makes sure to lift Araujo's shoulder or chest off the mat as she is doing this. Notice that the opponent is not flat on her stomach.

5. With her free hand, Harrison grabs her opponent's wrist and pulls it into her chest before tying up her arm.

6. With her free hand, Harrison feeds the bottom of Araujo's judo gi jacket into her left hand.

7. After tying the hand up, Harrison posts her right hand on the mat and kneels back.

8. She pulls Araujo toward her and then up on to her shoulder.

Continued on next page

9. Harrison keeps pulling Araujo back into the pin.

10. Harrison flattens herself out on her stomach, settling her weight onto her opponent's upper body.

TIE-UP SERIES: Connection to the Bent Armbar (Plan B)

1. When the first technique doesn't work, this is an option. Kayla Harrison begins by gaining wrist control, with Fernanda Araujo's palm facing down to the mat so she cannot grab her own gi or belt.

2. Araujo pulls her arm into her body and tries to grab her own gi or belt.

3. Harrison puts her bodyweight on her opponent and steps with her left leg (the same side as the wrist she has controlled) around toward the head.

4. She puts her knee on the mat trapping the opponent's head.

5. With her free hand, Harrison grabs Araujo's wrist and pulls it into her chest before tying up the arm.

6. With her free hand, Harrison feeds the bottom of the opponent's judo gi jacket into her left hand.

Continued on next page

7. After tying the hand up, Harrison posts her right hand on the mat and kneels back.

8. She pulls the opponent toward her and up onto her shoulder.

9. But what if she can't turn her opponent? When Harrison has wrist control, she slides her fingers down the opponent's hand to the end of the little finger.

10. Harrison rips the opponent's hand away from her gi, and with her other hand, Harrison grabs her own wrist and goes into a bent armbar (ude garame).

TIE-UP SERIES: Connection to the Choke (Plan C)

1. Kayla Harrison can apply this technique when she gets halfway through the move and has the wrist tied up, but her opponent is resisting too strongly and she cannot pull her onto her back. It begins with Harrison gaining wrist control, with the opponent's palm facing down to the mat.

2. Fernanda Araujo pulls her arm into her body and tries to grab her own gi or belt.

3. Harrison puts her bodyweight on Araujo.

4. Coming around the front of the opponent's body, Harrison pushes her head with her knee. Her elbow is in Araujo's back. Harrison's thumb is pushing up, lifting up the opponent's elbow. As she is doing this, Harrison makes sure to lift Araujo's shoulder or chest off the mat so she is not flat on her stomach.

Continued on next page

5. With her free hand, Harrison grabs her opponent's wrist and pulls into her chest before tying up the arm.

6. With her free hand, Harrison feeds the bottom of Araujo's judo gi jacket into the hand hooked through Araujo's arm—in this case, it's her left hand.

7. After Harrison has the opponent's arm tied up with the gi fed into one hand, she posts her free hand on the mat (in this example, the right hand) and kneels back.

8. Harrison pulls Araujo toward her and up onto her shoulder, but Harrison is stuck at this step, because although she has Araujo's arm tied up, the resistance is just too strong and Harrison cannot pull Araujo onto her back.

9. Harrison kneels back a step while pulling Araujo toward her. Harrison slides her hand down the opponent's neck on the lapel closest to her.

10. She drives her elbow toward the mat and begins choking.

11. Either Harrison will get the choke or Araujo will roll over and Harrison will get the pin.

COACHING TIP:
CORRECT KNEE PLACEMENT

In the previous chapter, we talked about having your arm on the side near you. The key to the tie-up series in all these moves is to make sure you keep your opponent's head in between your legs at all times. Refer to Step 4 in this series and note the position of the knee—it's right next to the opponent's head, preventing an escape in that direction.

TIE-UP SERIES: Opponent Resists by Trying to Get Up on All Fours (Plan D)

1. This option applies when one player has the opponent's wrist tied up but she is resisting strongly and cannot be pulled over. Instead of staying facedown on the mat resisting, the opponent tries to get up. Kayla Harrison begins by gaining wrist control.

2. Again, Fernanda Araujo pulls her arm into her body and tries to grab her own gi or belt.

3. Harrison puts her bodyweight on Araujo.

4. Coming around the front of the opponent's body, Harrison pushes her head with her knee. Her elbow is in Araujo's back. Her thumb is pushing up, lifting up Araujo's elbow. She makes sure to lift the opponent's shoulder or chest off the mat as she is doing this so that the opponent is not flat on her stomach.

5. With her free hand, Harrison grabs her opponent's wrist and pulls into her chest before tying up the arm.

6. With her free hand, Harrison feeds the bottom of the opponent's judo gi jacket into her left hand.

7. After Harrison has the opponent's arm tied up, she posts her right hand on the mat and kneels back.

8. Harrison pulls Araujo toward her and onto her shoulder.

Continued on next page

9. Harrison is stuck—she has Araujo's arm tied up, but Araujo is just too strong and cannot be pulled onto her back.

10. The opponent not only is resisting, but she is also up on her knees. Harrison steps around and gets her knee in front of the opponent's chest. Her other knee controls her head. Then Harrison takes her free arm and shoots it through the arm that she was trying to tie up.

11. Harrison cross-faces (biceps into the face) Araujo and drives her to the mat.

12. Harrison gets the pin.

COACHING TIP: THINK AHEAD

By now, you should be starting to see why opponents who do mat work with you feel like flies caught in a trap. The more they struggle the tighter they are caught. Some people watching a skilled judo player may believe the proficiency comes from something akin to Zen meditation that allows the successful *judoka* to know what the opponent is going to do before he or she does it. That's not the secret. It's just discipline and thinking ahead. We try to imagine every possible way an opponent can react and practice a move for that situation.

TIE-UP SERIES: Opponent Resists With Split Legs (Plan E)

1. This technique can be used when an opponent resists being turned over in another way—by splitting the legs apart. Bobby Lee begins by gaining wrist control.

2. He grabs the wrist and pulls Kayla Harrison's arm into her body. In this position, he should have his bodyweight on the opponent, stressing the opponent physically and mentally, as well as making escape more difficult. We repeat this point because it is one that so many people overlook.

Continued on next page

3. If Harrison splits her legs apart so that she can't be turned, Lee shifts his bodyweight back behind her butt, with his chest on it.

4. He reaches between her legs and grabs her belt.

5. Pulling up by the belt, Lee throws Harrison's bodyweight forward.

6. Key point: When he throws the opponent's bodyweight forward, he has to release the belt right away while always controlling her wrist.

7. As they go over, Lee slides back into an upper four-corner hold (kami shiho gatame).

TIE-UP SERIES: Alternate Armbar (Plan F)

1. This technique ends up in a different armbar—juji gatame (in judo), also known as the cross-body arm lock in grappling and mixed martial arts. It is used when the opponent is resisting so strongly that you cannot pull her over onto her back and she manages to get on her knees. As before, Kayla Harrison begins by gaining wrist control.

2. Fernanda Araujo pulls her arm into her body and tries to grab her own gi or belt.

Continued on next page

3. Harrison put her bodyweight on Araujo.

4. Coming around the front of Araujo's body, Harrison pushes her head with her knee. Her elbow is in Araujo's back. Her thumb is pushing up, lifting up the opponent's elbow. She makes sure to lift Araujo's shoulder or chest off the mat while she is doing this.

5. With her free hand, Harrison grabs her opponent's wrist and pulls into her chest before tying up the arm.

6. Harrison also uses her free hand to feed the bottom of the opponent's judo gi jacket into her left hand.

7. After Harrison has the opponent's arm tied up, she posts her free hand on the mat and kneels back.

8. Harrison pulls Araujo in and up onto her shoulder.

9. Once again, she is stuck. Harrison has the opponent's arm tied up, but the resistance is too strong and she cannot pull Araujo onto her back.

10. Araujo begins to get up on her hands and knees. Harrison anticipates that move while she is doing the tie-up, and when it happens, she puts a knee to the mat. (It should be the knee closest to the trapped arm, in this case, her right knee.) Now she has Araujo's head trapped between her knees.

Continued on next page

11. Harrison turns her body toward the opponent's hips while bringing her other knee over the back.

12. Harrison slides the knee on the ground underneath Araujo's face while reaping her head and rolling toward her back. It's key that she does this as the opponent is getting up so the momentum will carry her backward. She then reaps the head with her right leg to push the opponent backward.

13. A good judo player at this point will sense the danger and clasp both hands together to try to defend the armbar. With the opponent now on her back and her arm pinched tight between her knees, Harrison separates the arms. When doing juji gatame, the player should always pinch her knees together and control the opponent with her thighs. Harrison makes sure she locks the arm against her body while trying to separate the arms. One way to do this is by grabbing her own gi. When ripping out to apply the arm lock, she leans toward the opponent's head.

14. Harrison locks the arm against her body and lifts her hips to apply the arm lock. She positions her forearm near Araujo's wrist for more leverage.

TIE-UP SERIES: Triangle Choke (Plan G)

1. This technique, sankaku jime (in judo), also known as the triangle choke in grappling and mixed martial arts, is used when the steps are the same as in plan F, but at the last minute, the opponent pulls her arm down and away. As before, Kayla Harrison begins by gaining wrist control, with the opponent's palm facing down to the mat.

2. Fernanda Araujo pulls her arm into her body and tries to grab her own gi or belt.

3. Harrison puts her bodyweight on her opponent.

4. Coming around the front of the opponent's body, Harrison pushes her head with her knee. Her elbow is in Araujo's back. Harrison's thumb is pushing up, lifting up the opponent's elbow. She makes sure to lift Araujo's shoulder or chest off the mat as she is doing this.

Continued on next page

5. While Harrison is doing the tie-up, her opponent gets up to her base. As Araujo does this, Harrison steps over and goes into a sankaku as they are getting up. With her free hand, she grabs her opponent's wrist and pulls into her chest.

6. If her opponent manages to pull the arm down, Harrison falls to the side opposite the arm she has controlled, pulling up on that arm and pulling the opponent with her.

7. The key to sankaku is extending both legs out at the same time. This will automatically put Harrison's bottom leg under Araujo's head, where it should be, instead of getting that leg trapped under her back. (This problem happens for many people if they don't extend their legs.) This also will position Harrison's top leg to catch Araujo's arm.

8. Harrison feeds the bottom of the judo gi jacket into the hand with which she has hooked Araujo's arm. This will allow Harrison to control Araujo's arm with just one hand. When doing sankaku, Harrison should be pinching her thighs together to control the opponent's body.

9. Harrison hooks her top leg under her own bottom leg at the knee to form a figure-4. She uses her free arm to pull the opponent's free arm in tight and across the face. Harrison brings the heel of the bottom leg toward herself and squeezes her legs to complete the choke.

SHORTER SERIES

Whereas the tie-up series has seven different variations, each with many steps, there are several series involving fewer techniques. Not all series are equally complicated. This series begins with the player on top attempting an armbar. If that doesn't work, the next step is to do a different armbar (plan B), and if the opponent successfully resists that attempt, then the player moves into a pin (plan C). The sit-out choke is another example of a shorter series.

SHORTER SERIES: Armbar to Pin, From the Bottom

1. Aaron Kunihiro is on the bottom, and the opponent, Tyler Yonemori, is in between his legs. Kunihiro grabs both his opponent's forearms.

2. Kunihiro spins to his right (a 90-degree turn) and grabs the opponent's inner thigh with his right arm. Kunihiro's left leg goes over Yonemori's head.

3. Using the power in his legs, Kunihiro rolls the opponent on his back and sits up.

4. Kunihiro grabs his gi with his left hand. He makes sure his forearm is on the wrist of the arm he is trying to arm-lock. He leans toward Yonemori's head and rips his arm free to secure the arm lock.

5. Holding the opponent's wrist against his chest with both hands, Kunihiro arches upward with his hips to apply the armbar.

SHORTER SERIES: Armbar to Pin, From the Bottom (Plan B)

1. This series begins when Aaron Kunihiro is on the bottom and the opponent, Tyler Yonemori, is in between his legs. Kunihiro grabs both his opponent's forearms.

2. Kunihiro spins to his right (a 90-degree turn) and grabs the opponent's inner thigh with his right arm. Kunihiro's left leg goes over Yonemori's head.

3. Kunihiro uses the power in his legs to roll the opponent on his back and sit up.

4. This is when plan B diverges from the previous series. Yonemori pulls his right arm away and turns into Kunihiro, thinking that Kunihiro can't get the armbar.

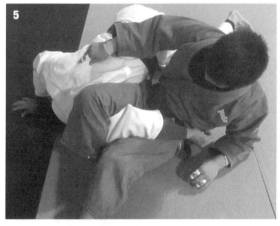

5. Kunihiro spins and brings his right leg over his other arm and posts his left arm so he can sit up.

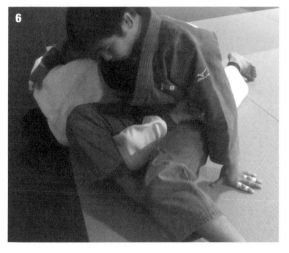

6. He leans his bodyweight forward and gets the bent-arm lock.

Continued on next page

7. He anticipates the opponent's next move ... Yonemori will have to do a somersault to escape the arm lock.

8. When Yonemori hits the mat ...

9. ... Kunihiro leans forward and secures a pin. Although a pin will not finish a match in mixed martial arts, this pin will win a judo match and score points in sambo, grappling or jiu-jitsu.

SHORTER SERIES: Armbar to Pin, From the Top

1. In an attempt to prevent Tyler Yonemori from getting either a half nelson or wrist control, Janine Nakao may grab Yonemori's leg. (Usually when players get this move, it is because they have been trying to get another move and been unsuccessful.) Yonemori puts his leg into position as "bait," trying to entice his opponent to take it so he can try for the arm lock.

2. Yonemori moves his leg to start to straighten the arm out. As he is doing that, he is putting all his weight on Nakao and putting his pelvis on her, attempting to flatten her out.

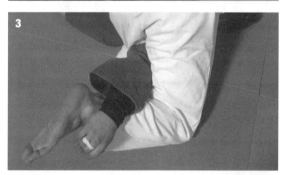

3. When Yonemori is beside his opponent doing mat work and his opponent grabs his ankle, Yonemori automatically extends that leg, puts his pelvis on Nakao's elbow, lifts up with his ankle and applies the arm lock by putting his bodyweight on her arm.

4. Yonemori scissors his legs at the ankle and arches his hips to apply pressure on the arm. Note: Examine the photo in Step 3 again. Yonemori should be pressing his pelvis into her elbow while lifting her wrist up with his leg, trying to secure an arm lock.

SHORTER SERIES: Armbar to Pin, From the Top (Plan B)

1. As in the previous series, Tyler Yonemori, on top, is trying to do mat work. While Yonemori is attempting to get a mat move, Janine Nakao, on the bottom, grabs Yonemori's ankle.

2. Yonemori moves his leg to start to straighten the arm out. As he is doing that, he is putting all his weight on his opponent and putting his pelvis on her, attempting to flatten her out.

3. Again, Yonemori starts to straighten his legs to apply the armbar.

4. While Yonemori is applying the original arm lock—before he can get the armbar—Nakao resists by letting go of the leg and bending her arm in the opposite direction, grabbing Yonemori's other leg.

5. Yonemori switches hips and hooks the arm by immediately bringing his outside leg underneath the elbow and turning toward Nakao's feet. He brings his other leg in the opposite direction toward her head.

6. Yonemori straightens out Nakao's arm while keeping pressure on the elbow. The top leg is used to hook the opponent's arm to secure the arm lock.

SHORTER SERIES: Armbar to Pin, From the Top (Plan C)

1. As in the previous two series, Tyler Yonemori, on top, is trying to do mat work. While he is attempting to get a mat move, Janine Nakao, on the bottom, grabs his ankle.

2. Yonemori moves his leg to start to straighten the arm out. As he is doing that, he is putting all his weight on his opponent and putting his pelvis on her, attempting to flatten her out.

3. Again, Yonemori starts to straighten his legs to apply the armbar.

4. Sometimes when a player applies the armbar, the opponent will not tap. This usually will happen if the opponent has grabbed the near leg higher up close to the knee. Here, Yonemori takes advantage of the opponent's grip on him. He posts his right arm on the mat. He brings the leg that the opponent has grabbed over her back and traps her arm behind her back. He keeps walking in a circle until he rolls her over to a pin.

5. As Yonemori puts Nakao on her back, he keeps the arm hooked in his leg for a tighter pin. He reaches under the other arm, driving his armpit into her face.

SHORTER SERIES: Sit-Out Choke to Pin

1. As Riley McIlwain begins this move, his outside leg is to the side and in front, nearly even with Tyler Yonemori's head.

2. McIlwain secures his front hand deep underneath the opponent's chin on the collar.

3. With his inside leg, McIlwain steps forward as far as possible and flattens Yonemori onto his stomach. Note that McIlwain's elbow is pinching against the side of Yonemori's neck and head. McIlwain's chest should be pressing down on the opponent's head. To complete the choke, all McIlwain needs to do is pull the lapel that he has with his right arm and continue lifting his elbow toward the ceiling. He doesn't arch his back to try to complete the choke. (That is the biggest mistake most people make.) He has his chest on Yonemori's head, pushing it down and adding pressure to aid the choke.

SHORTER SERIES: Sit-Out Choke to Pin (Plan B)

1. What if the opponent is not tapping? Some people just have a freakishly strong neck and are almost impossible to choke. In that case, it's time for plan B. As Riley McIlwain begins this move, his outside leg is to the side and in front, nearly even with Tyler Yonemori's head.

2. McIlwain secures his front hand deep underneath the opponent's chin on the collar.

3. With his inside leg, McIlwain steps forward as far as possible and flattens Yonemori onto his stomach. If the opponent is not tapping at this point, either McIlwain did not grasp the lapel in far enough or the opponent is freakishly strong-necked. McIlwain will go on to plan B.

Continued on next page

4. McIlwain springs forward in the sit-out, his inside leg coming as far forward as possible. If he is doing the choke correctly, Yonemori should be tapping before the sit-out is finished.

5. If the opponent still hasn't tapped, McIlwain will use the arm that was beside Yonemori's head to underhook his arm.

Authors' Note: Although we have these steps listed separately, the moves are really done very quickly, especially the last two, so they look as if they are all done at the same time. They are, in fact, done so close together that they are almost simultaneous. They are broken down here separately for demonstration purposes only.

6. McIlwain steps behind with his outside leg.

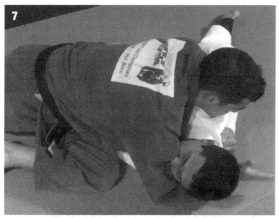

7. He lets go of the choke and does a cross-face with his right arm.

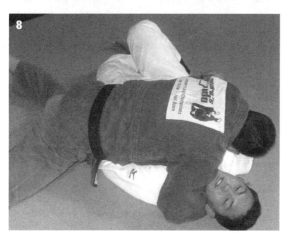

8. McIlwain uses his body to drive Yonemori onto his back into the pin.

COACHING TIP:
MAT WORK IS A FEEL

The situation drills and techniques in this chapter represent tried-and-true methods that we use all the time.

This is my philosophy: If you can do a good armbar and get everyone with it, that doesn't make you a good mat person. Mat work is more than being good at one technique. Mat work is a feel. If you do these drills all the time, you develop a feel. You know where your opponent is going before he goes there.

I drilled my son, Jimmy Jr., when he was 5 years old. He did these drills continuously, moving from one pin to another, from one technique to another. Before I worked out, I had him and his sister, Tanya, do all these drills with me so they had to anticipate where I was going.

When Jimmy was older, whether he was wrestling or doing judo, he could feel his opponent. They couldn't believe that he knew where they were going before they knew where they were going.

In most contests, when people are on the mat, they don't usually get that one technique they are trying. They end up letting their opponent up and giving them a chance to beat them standing. I believe competitors are better off having a sequence of techniques they can go to from the first technique. If they are almost continually on the opponent, making progress, moving from one technique attempt to another, the referee will allow them to continue mat work rather than stopping the match and making the competitors restart from the standing position.

If a competitor is doing one technique, he should know his opponent's options for escaping from that technique. If he has been practicing, he can automatically go to the second technique and beat his opponent. It doesn't mean he must be robotic. It's like doing standing combinations—these are just combinations in mat work that must be practiced.

An American System

Outside the United States, judo players may do mat work three hours every night with 30 different people. They can develop a feel for mat work that way.

In America—certainly across most of the country—players don't have three hours a night practicing with other people in order to develop that feel on the mat. If they only have an hour and a half three times a week, they need to take advantage of that time. A system lends itself to greater efficiency. That can be done by setting up situations.

The Mat-Work Series

In a training book, such as this, techniques should be portrayed as technically correct and perfect in every photo as much as possible. This is why we took some of the same pictures over two or three times. Of course, you realize as a competitor and a coach that not every technique will be done perfectly every time in competition or in practice. However, when people who are not so experienced are reading our book, they may not know the right way to do a technique. In this chapter, we have endeavored to show the technically "perfect" technique.

In later chapters, you may notice that some techniques are not done in the standard way. That is, they don't look technically perfect. In those cases, we've pointed this out and explained why we included the technique the way it is being done.

—*James Pedro Sr.*

Editor's Note: Jimmy Pedro Jr. earned gold at the 1999 World Judo Championships. He was also a four-time Olympic team member and two-time Olympic bronze medalist. He coached 2012 Olympic gold-medalist Kayla Harrison. Tanya Pedro Falco was, at age 15, one of the youngest ever to win the U.S. Open Judo Championships.

CHAPTER 5

MAT-WORK COUNTERS

Mat-work counters are the simplest example of training for situations. Your opponent attempts a technique on you and you counter it (as opposed to transitions from standing to mat work, mat-work combinations, training for situations and mat-work series—all of which involve you initiating the move). Many judo books discuss counters to throws, but most of those books pay very little attention to mat-work counters. In Chapter 1, we briefly explored mat-work counters and discussed a technique we use with beginning students. Here, we give more examples, from basic to advanced.

COUNTER TO AN ATTEMPTED HEAD-LOCK (KOSHI GURUMA) THROW FROM THE KNEES

We start with a very basic counter from the position on the following page, which is very common with beginners in judo. Both players are on their knees, trying to get the other in a head lock, and turning and throwing into a pin. In this situation, usually the stronger (or larger) person is going to win. If the smaller person suddenly changes direction to go with the turn, that person will end up on top. Here is a simple move demonstrating the idea of a mat-work counter, using the example of countering an attempted throw from the knees.

Of course, this counter could be done just as easily by the larger player, or by either of two players of the same size. We teach it early on to beginners to demonstrate that a couple of basic judo concepts of maximum efficiency with minimum effort and using the other person's force against him or her apply equally well on the mat as when using standing techniques.

COUNTER TO AN ATTEMPTED HEAD-LOCK (KOSHI GURUMA) THROW FROM THE KNEES

1. Both players are on their knees and have a grip on each other's sleeve with one hand and a high grip on the collar with the other. Both are pulling down with their left.

2. Ronda Rousey, the smaller player, quickly reverses the direction by pulling to the right, to go with the opponent (Crystal Butts).

3. As the larger player is off-balance, the smaller player drives her bodyweight into her ...

4. ... to put her on her back in a pin (kesa gatame, in this example).

COUNTER TO A REVERSE TRIANGLE CHOKE (REVERSE SANKAKU JIME)

Many matches are won by a set of techniques called a *sankaku jime* and reverse sankaku jime in judo and a triangle choke or reverse triangle choke in mixed martial arts and jiu-jitsu. In both, the top player uses a figure-4 to trap one arm and choke the opponent with his or her legs, leaving both hands free to either trap the opposite arm for a better pin or attempt an arm lock. It is a bad position for the player on the bottom.

Because not everyone is familiar with these techniques, which is one of the reasons that they work, we will first explain a reverse sankaku jime and then describe the counter for it.

As you read through the steps in the counter, keep this important point in mind: For this technique to work, put the back of your hand against your opponent's knee as he or she steps in. With your other hand, cup the opponent's heel. Do not grab either leg. You want to lull your opponent into a sense of security. If you do not have a grip anywhere and your opponent almost has a figure-4 sunk in, he or she will feel confident. Your opponent will roll to one side expecting to lock in the pin and choke you.

REVERSE TRIANGLE CHOKE (REVERSE SANKAKU)

1. This demonstrates a reverse triangle to Janine Nakao's right side. She begins standing beside Aaron Kunihiro, with her right hand on the inside collar behind his neck and her left hand on his belt. She steps in front of the opponent and pulls forward with both hands, opening him up so there is a space between his elbow and knee.

2. Nakao hooks her foot inside behind the arm in that space she just opened up. After she gets her foot inside behind the arm, she drops her other foot beside Kunihiro's head trying to touch the heel of her foot to her other knee. Note: The key to all types of sankaku is pinching the thighs together and controlling the opponent's upper body, something that most people forget to do.

3. As she drops down to her side, she stays on her elbow. She does not flatten the opponent out. Her upper leg should be starting to catch his arm while her bottom leg is stretching underneath the opponent.

4. When she is working on this side, she switches and puts her right foot under her left knee. (If she's working the opposite side, she puts her left foot under her right knee.)

5. After Nakao has secured her knee, she reaches down and grabs her ankle or foot and pulls her knee in tighter.

6. After she has secured the arm and her foot is tight into her knee, she drives her pelvis flat into Kunihiro, arches and stretches him out.

7. Once the opponent is stretched out, she rolls him and secures the pin.

COUNTER TO A REVERSE SANKAKU

1. Crystal Butts puts a knee into Ronda Rousey's shoulder and hooks her arm with the other leg.

2. Rousey puts one hand against the opponent's knee and the other cups the heel.

Demonstration Rousey is sitting up just to show how the hand is placed on the opponent's heel.

3. Feeling confident, her opponent falls to the side, thinking she can pin her.

4. As her opponent rolls, Rousey spreads her hands apart as far as they can go. The result is that Butts is lying on her back with her legs spread wide apart. Not a very defensible position. (Note: When she is resisting, the opponent applying sankaku is going to pull harder to roll her. The harder the pull, the easier it is to roll fast right up into the opponent.)

Why this counter works

Why this counter works Rousey has her hands on Butts' knee and heel, and when she spreads her arms, it results in an awkward position for Butts. Some students ask whether spreading the arms apart leaves one vulnerable to an armbar. The answer is demonstrated in this photo: The person on the bottom is in no position to execute an armbar.

5. Rousey continues the direction of the roll so that she is lying on her stomach, with one hand under her opponent's neck grabbing the collar. She slides the hand that was on the knee underneath, grabbing under the opponent's shoulder.

6. Now that's a much nicer position for Rousey, isn't it?

SIT-OUT ARMBAR COUNTER TO TURNOVER

1. When Crystal Butts reaches over Ronda Rousey's back attempting a turnover, Rousey, from this position, grabs Butts' wrist, pulls it into her body and overhooks her arm.

2. Rousey drops her weight.

3. She sits out toward the opponent's hips.

4. She pulls up on the wrist while putting her weight on Butts' elbow. At this position, Rousey has an arm lock.

5. If Butts is up on her hands and knees, Rousey, who is applying an arm lock, should anticipate that Butts would do a forward roll to escape.

6. If Butts tries a forward roll to escape the armbar, Rousey keeps the overhooked arm locked tight against her body, sits forward putting her weight across Butts' abdomen and grabs her hips, pulling in. The locked arm and her weight across the lower body prevents an escape by an inside turn, and her arm on the outside blocks an outside turn.

SIT-OUT ARMBAR COUNTER TO TURNOVER, PIN COMBINATION NO. 2

1. A second option for this counter is to continue turning into a reverse scarf hold (ushiro kesa gatame). Ronda Rousey locks Crystal Butts' arm to her body and rolls hard to her right.

2. Rousey helps her opponent's rollover by lifting with her left elbow, keeping Butts' arm still locked under her right arm.

3. She rolls on top of Butts.

4. Rousey keeps the right arm locked against her body as she turns toward her opponent's hips, keeping all her weight on the opponent's torso.

SIT-OUT ARMBAR COUNTER TO FRONT TURNOVER

1. In this example, the opponent, Meghan Arena, is on top but in front of Hana Carmichael. In international judo matches, this is a common turnover attempt. The top player is attempting to reach through and grab both lapels. Arena attempts a turnover from the front. With head to hips, she has reached across Carmichael's back, underneath her left arm.

2. Carmichael must make sure she gets her head out from underneath her opponent's body. She reaches up above the opponent's elbow, locking the arm tight against her body with her left arm while she steps forward with her left leg. She uses her right arm to post, placing her right hand about even with her left foot so that she is not off-balance. (Otherwise, her opponent can pull her backward.) As she steps through, all her weight is going in the direction of her opponent's hips while her opponent's weight is going in the opposite direction. Note that she is in this position for less than a second. Obviously, we have broken it down frame by frame for demonstration purposes. She doesn't want to remain in this position with her arm straight.

3. Carmichael steps through with her right leg, doing a sit-out. She is really sitting through, so far that her head is now on her opponent's back. Note how far forward her right leg has come and now her weight is on her elbow. (She is no longer posting her hand on the mat with a straight arm.)

Continued on next page

4. With her right hand, Carmichael pulls up on Arena's wrist and leans all her bodyweight on the opponent's elbow. This is painful for the opponent.

5. The opponent's only possible chance of escape is a forward roll. Carmichael holds on to that arm as Arena rolls over.

6. As Arena comes over to her back, Carmichael turns toward her hips so that her stomach is on the mat. She spreads her legs to give herself a wide base.

7. Carmichael slides her right hand under Arena's leg to stop her from turning to escape.

COACHING TIP:
JUDO TECHNIQUES DO TRANSLATE TO NO-GI SITUATIONS

Common sense doesn't seem to be all that common. We find that most people automatically assume that the techniques they see demonstrated in judo don't work in no-*gi* situations. Even though the last few techniques in this chapter are performed in judo gi, they did not involve any grabbing of the uniform and could be done just as well by athletes competing in grappling and mixed martial arts. If you realize this, then you are ahead of the game.

If judo transfers so easily to mixed martial arts and grappling—as we believe it does, and we can point to some of our students who have been very successful as proof of that—then why don't we see a massive number of judo players dominating in the UFC? There are several possible explanations. First, most judo players do not focus on mat work. Ronda Rousey, for example, though, is the Strikeforce world champion and an Olympic and world medalist in judo because she was one of those players who *did* focus on winning on the ground.

A second point that ought to be obvious to anyone who watches a lot of matches in any combat sport is that most people attack from only a very few positions. *Jiu-jitsu* players, for example, seem to be continually trying to be "in the guard." Some jiu-jitsu instructors tell us that they prefer that position because it is the easiest to defend and attack from. There is nothing wrong with the guard position in itself. (We demonstrate a number of attacks from the guard in this book.). Our objection is relying too much on any one position.

The last few counters in this chapter all begin with one player on the bottom and her opponent attacking her. Very few people attack from the bottom position. It is safe to say that most often when someone is on the bottom on all fours with the opponent on his or her back, the person on the bottom is defending. Learning counters that allow an attack from the bottom position has a couple of advantages. One is that the opponent generally will not expect an attack from there. Because most people are only defensive when they are in the bottom position, the opponent may feel pretty confident and not as ready for an attack as he or she otherwise might be.

We also emphasize learning to attack from the bottom, countering the opponent, for the "sneak attack" factor. Once a player is recognized for winning on the ground, he or she is going to need to lull opponents into a false sense of security. If a player is an accomplished mat technician, the competition will know that and will have been told by their coaches to try to keep the match standing.

At the time this book went to press, Rousey had won 100 percent of her MMA matches by armbar. Yet in the 2012 Strikeforce world title fight, Miesha Tate went to the mat with Rousey. Why? You'd assume that someone who had won a world title, as Tate had, was not a stupid person or an inexperienced competitor. So why would she end up on the mat? Because she was on Rousey's back and felt confident that she was the attacker. Then Rousey reversed positions and armbarred her.

Here's the lesson: Learn to fight from the bottom position!

CHAPTER 6

DRILL THE RIGHT WAY TO WIN ON THE GROUND (HOW TO BE DANGEROUS ON THE MAT)

If you've been paying attention, you've no doubt noticed that many of the techniques we have shown so far look pretty much alike. There is a reason for this: They *are* pretty much alike. The secret to winning on the ground is connections. In fact, we were going to call this book *Mat-Work Connections,* but our editors suggested *Winning on the Ground* because, they pointed out, no one would know what we meant by mat-work connections unless they read the book, and people usually don't buy books when they don't understand what they are about. Everyone knows what winning on the ground means, and most people want to do it.

Mat-work connections are the secret to winning on the ground. You connect several techniques that you do very well, linking them in ways that are a little different each time. So if your opponent blocks your half nelson by putting a hand out, you grab the wrist and do the wrist-control series. If he or she is on top of you, you can "collect the arm," go into the mount (either pin in judo or start punching in mixed martial arts) and then execute the armbar. If your opponent rolls to his or her stomach to escape the armbar, go for the half nelson.

The diagram illustrates why it is not as easy to avoid an armbar as some people think. This is an example of three different techniques and the end being an armbar.

1. **Throw—Mount—Turnover** ⟶
2. **Throw—Turnover—Mount** ⟶
3. **Turnover—Mount—Throw** ⟶
4. **Throw** ⟶
5. **Turnover—Mount** ⟶

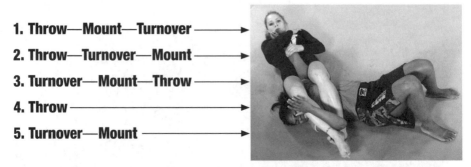

Let's say you only know three moves to set up an armbar: throwing your opponent to her back and then doing an armbar; being on top of your opponent in the mount to an armbar or a turnover from your back; and throwing your leg over to an armbar. Five different options are shown in the diagram (and three of those are discussed here), but there are actually many more.

OPTIONS

In Option 1 (shown in the photos), you could throw your opponent, then do the mount, and if your opponent managed to roll you over to the bottom, you could do the turnover to armbar. You could do the throw, and if that misses, try the turnover. If that misses, go into the mount and try the armbar from there. That's Option 2. You could start out in the turnover— maybe your opponent missed a throw and ended up on the bottom so you went for the turnover. Then you tried the mount, couldn't get that, gave up, went back to standing, threw your opponent and then transitioned to the armbar. That's Option 3.

OPTION 1

1. Ronda Rousey begins by throwing Travis McLaughlin.

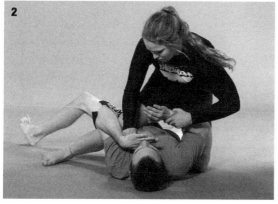

2. She tries an armbar but misses. Her second transition begins from the mount.

Continued on next page

3. McLaughlin escapes from that, too.

4. He turns and gets on top of Rousey. She goes to a third technique—a turnover from the bottom to an armbar. (A few choices were demonstrated in Chapter 2.)

PRACTICE BOTH SIDES

One thing we hope this book teaches you is that you should always learn every technique on both sides. So you don't have just those possibilities because you should be able to do them to the right side as well as to the left. And you don't have to always do the three options together. You could throw and jump into the armbar—that's another possible option. That is, performing each move individually (throw, mount, turnover) gives you three more options. Or you could do combinations of any two of them. That is why we said there were many more than five possibilities. In fact, because you can do the same move in a sequence more than once, there is an infinite number. (For example, you can throw, go to the mount, roll over, try the armbar and then roll back on top in the mount.)

To illustrate further, an interviewer once asked Rousey, "You've won eight matches in a row in the first round using an armbar, including the world title. What are you going to do if one day you can't get that armbar in the first round?"

She shrugged and answered, "I guess I'd probably try it again in the second round."

There are two points here that explain why we are showing the same thing several different times, but each time is a little different. First, when you train, your mat techniques should be connected. Second, if you do train the connections between techniques, you can vary those paths so that no matter which way your opponent turns, it all ends up with you winning.

PUTTING THE BUILDING BLOCKS TOGETHER

When Rousey was young, she did the tomoe nage armbar that we showed in Chapter 2. When she was 16, she spent a few years training with the Pedros. Jimmy Pedro Jr. was famous for a different armbar entry in which he grabbed the far leg of his opponent and pulled it around his head. After her time with the Pedros, when she was asked to do an armbar for a photo shoot, she did the one demonstrated on the following pages. Although it looks extremely complicated, the first seven steps are the exact tomoe nage armbar with an escape attempt that appears in Chapter 2. When she began to train with the Pedros, she was essentially learning this move at Step 8 because she already had the first part down. She had the building blocks in place, so it had been easy for her to add to them with the second armbar entry.

If you have several good mat techniques that fit together, opponents will find it almost impossible to fight off your attacks indefinitely. You literally leave your opponent nowhere to turn. Winning becomes inevitable. But if it's that simple, then why don't more people do it? If you find yourself asking that question, look at the following armbar sequence. Does it look simple to you?

It's a lot of work, not just for a day or every day for a year but every day for 14 years. It's also a lot of working smart. When Rousey went to the Pedros, she was the No. 1-ranked woman in the United States and had never lost to an American at her weight. For the next six years, until she retired from judo competition, she never lost to an American and lost to very few outside the United States. Most athletes in her situation don't try to add new techniques to their repertoire. We have heard it a thousand times: "I must be doing something right. I'm on the Olympic team/national champion/junior national champion/best at the YMCA."

Our point is that most athletes who have the first seven steps in this sequence down and are winning international matches would not think it necessary to connect another technique or two to it. They would just train harder using the techniques that had made them a success to that point. Most people don't make mat-work connections, but they should because that would be training not just harder but smarter.

PUTTING THE BUILDING BLOCKS TOGETHER

1. Ronda Rousey begins with a right standard grip: right hand on Travis McLaughlin's lapel and left hand on the sleeve.

2. She puts her right foot on his left leg above the knee.

3. She lets go of the lapel with her right hand and grabs the sleeve (or the wrist).

4. She pushes with her foot placed above the opponent's knee. As his leg gets pushed away from her, his arm will be straightened out.

5. To escape the armbar, McLaughlin may try to roll his arm so that instead of his elbow being to the side, it is now pointing up toward the ceiling. He has now twisted out of the armbar.

6. She keeps hold of his arm and turns with him. Refer to Step 4. Notice that Rousey was on her side and her opponent's elbow was turned to the side. When he turned, she turned with him and now she is facedown, and she still has his elbow locked tight against her body.

7. If she can stop his roll, she'll lock his arm to her body and do a one-handed push-up from the floor. This puts her pelvis directly on his elbow. She arches her hips to complete the armbar.

Continued on next page

8. Here begins the second part of this technique. If she cannot get the armbar and her opponent starts to pull away to jerk his arm out, she keeps hold of it with her left arm.

9. With her legs still on either side of his arm, Rousey turns toward McLaughlin's hips.

10. As she turns, she grabs his arm with her right arm, as well, and slides her arms up to his wrist and takes the straight armbar from that position. (Note: This is a continuation from Step 9, but with photos taken from the opposite side because she has now turned toward his hips.)

11. If she is not quick enough to get the straight armbar when she switched positions and he pulls his arm in so that she can no longer extend his arm, she grabs her own thigh, high, with her left hand, trying to keep his arm as far away from his body as possible.

12. Rousey keeps McLaughlin's arm held tightly to her body with her left arm.

13. She reaches out with her right arm and grabs his far leg, preferably at the ankle, if she can reach it.

14. She rotates his legs in a circular motion over her head while her inside leg lifts his upper torso high in the air.

15. Even before he hits the mat, she should be sitting up, continuing to push him down with a leg across his torso.

Continued on next page

16. By the time his back is on the mat, her other leg comes over his body. She pinches her knees together.

17. While keeping tension on the opponent's right arm at all times, she drives her left arm through as far as possible and grabs her own gi. She leans toward his head while trying to pull his arms apart.

18. When Rousey has ripped McLaughlin's arm free and has it tight to her body, she flattens out and does the juji gatame arm lock by arching her hips to apply pressure on his elbow.

CHAPTER 7

BASIC MAT-WORK DRILL TRAINING

A coach once told me, "I know all 67 throws in the go kyu no waza." He was upset when I confessed:

   1. *"I don't know if it is actually spelled 'go kyu no waza.'"*

   2. *"I don't know if there are actually 67 throws in it." (Jim Pedro Sr. says there were 40 throws in the original gokyo no waza syllabus of standard judo throws. Now there are 67.)*

   3. *"I certainly can't do all of them."*

The coach walked away shaking his head at me, a sixth-degree black belt.

—AnnMaria De Mars

Part of that coach's disbelief might be that his view of what it means to "be able to do a technique" differs from mine.

Being a good judo competitor, or a good coach, is not a matter of knowing every possible technique. In fact, being familiar with too many techniques might actually put you at a disadvantage. For example, in a match, one player attempts a throw and misses because the opponent steps out of the way or pushes the opponent down. Both players hesitate, and in the end, nothing happens. The referee stops the match and stands the player up, or the bottom player flattens out or turtles up in defense and then the referee stops the match. It becomes a lost opportunity. Either player would have been better off if he or she had been able to react without hesitation with one well-learned move.

Another lost opportunity occurs when a player is almost pinned, almost armbarred and has no idea how to escape. The key to hitting those opportunities is practice. It is drilling not 67 moves but a few that work in crucial situations.

WHAT'S A DRILL?

That might seem like a silly question, but we ask it because we disagree with what some people consider drills. The mat-work series we discussed in the earlier chapters are all done with a partner who is cooperating to some extent. The partner may be putting up resistance as you go for the armbar or may pull the arm out when you go for wrist control. The key point in all these previous examples is you knew what your partner was going to do and your partner knew what you were going to do. Your partner was going to reach over, you were going to lock his or her arm under your armpit and step out, and so on. You do repetitions until the techniques are automatic. What are speed drills then? We think speed drills are misnamed. They are just fast repetitions.

We consider real mat-work drills to be situation drills. A drill has three parts.

1. It begins with a situation that occurs in competition. For example, one person has just been thrown and the thrower is very close, about to attempt a pin, choke or arm lock.

2. There is an objective. This can be to escape an armbar, to pin the opponent or to get away from the opponent and stand up.

3. Neither partner knows what the other one is going to do.

How is a drill different from sparring or free practice? Drills are usually shorter, for one thing. The main difference, though, is the objective of a drill is usually more specific, and that's important. It's not very likely that you are equally good at all parts of mat work. Choosing the right drill allows you to focus just on those areas that you really want to improve. So we begin our drills with an area almost everybody needs to improve: escapes.

INSIDE-TURN ESCAPE DRILL

Have you ever seen a situation in which one player is on his back, maybe he just got thrown or the other player managed to turn him over, and just at the last second, the player on the bottom turns out and escapes? Did you think that maybe the other player practiced for just that situation? Here is a drill we do at all levels, from young kids to black belts.

Scarf-Hold Escape A player who is not very experienced will usually try to do a scarf hold *(kesa gatame)*. This isn't the strongest pin in judo, but it is one of the easier ones to get. That said, it can be effective. Rousey won a match in the 2004 Olympics by pinning Sarah Clark of Great Britain with a kesa gatame. It is one of those techniques that work for kids in the 6-year-old novice divisions on up through international competitors, so it is the judo equivalent of a free throw in basketball—something you learn at the very beginning and try to perfect throughout your career. Just as important is learning to escape from it.

What You'll Learn From This Drill There are four things to take away from this drill. First is how to do an inside turn, second is to react quickly, third is to do the right escape for a given position, and fourth is, as an attacker, to learn the best position on the mat.

The drill is only 10 seconds, then the players switch positions. Giving only 10 seconds forces both players to react quickly to take advantage of an opportunity to win or to escape. In a large group, do this drill once, with each player taking a turn on the back, and then switch partners. With a smaller group, when there are only a few partners of the same size, you may want to do this drill several times with the same person before switching.

This is a good drill for learning how to get out of a dangerous position and also for developing a feel for mat work. After turning away from the opponent and getting pinned several times, gradually the player will get into the habit of turning toward the inside on a scarf hold.

INSIDE-TURN ESCAPE DRILL: Moves for the Bottom Player

1. Start with the player on the top almost securing the pin. Notice that Manny Gamburyan has not yet tightened his grip around Ronda Rousey's head or pulled her left arm into him very tightly. At this point, he is 90 percent of the way into the pin. Notice that Rousey, as the player on the bottom, has done one thing correctly right away: She has put one hand up to defend and make some space between herself and her opponent. The best choice for the bottom player in this position, with the opponent coming toward her for a scarf hold (kesa gatame), is an inside turn. (Turn inside toward the opponent.)

Continued on next page

2. When the coach yells "Go!" the players have 10 seconds to either get the pin or escape. As soon as the coach says "Go!" Gamburyan turns his body hard toward Rousey and pulls that left shoulder back. This is the same move as the "shrimp crawl" exercise that is done in so many clubs. From this position, the inside turn—pulling in the shoulder that's farther from the opponent and turning toward the opponent—is the most likely chance to escape. Rousey keeps her elbows in close to her body. She doesn't want to give her opponent a chance to arm-bar her. The key here is for the bottom player to move as fast as possible to turn out of the pin before the top player can tighten it.

3. Rousey continues to turn onto her stomach.

4. Once she gets to her stomach, Rousey gets up on her knees and backs up, moving at an angle away from Gamburyan. If she were to back straight out, it would be easier for her opponent to do a half nelson. Then Rousey attacks. It doesn't matter with what technique. The goal isn't to escape; the goal is to win. To repeat, the key here is for the bottom player to move as fast as possible to turn out of the pin before the top player can tighten it — and then attack. Remember that.

INSIDE-TURN ESCAPE DRILL: Moves for the Top Player (Other Perspective)

1. Ronda Rousey, the player on the top, is as close as possible to Crystal Butts without yet touching.

2. When the coach yells "Go!" the players have 10 seconds to either get the pin or escape. Immediately, Rousey drives in.

3. She secures the pin.

OUTSIDE-TURN ESCAPE DRILL AND VARIATION

The side mount *(yoko shiho gatame)* is a stronger hold than the scarf hold. As players gain experience, they give up on the scarf hold and try different pins, like the side hold, when they are offered the opportunity to get "any position close to the opponent."

More experienced players will usually choose to start in a position for a side hold. A variation on that is an upper four-corner hold *(kami shiho gatame)*. This position is even more advantageous than starting from the side.

OUTSIDE-TURN ESCAPE DRILL: From Side Hold (Yoko Shiho Gatame)

1. Crystal Butts is on the bottom. Ronda Rousey, the player on the top, is as close as possible to her without touching. Notice that Butts has done one thing correctly right away: She has put her right hand under the opponent's armpit to make some space. The best choice for Butts in this position, with Rousey across her body, is an outside turn. (Turn outside away from the opponent.) Being an experienced mat technician, Butts knows that and is already preparing to turn in that direction.

2. When the coach yells "Go!" the players have 10 seconds to either get the pin or escape. Butts immediately turns her body hard, away from Rousey, and pulls that left shoulder back. This move is the same as the "shrimp crawl" exercise that is done in so many clubs. In this position—the outside turn—pulling in the shoulder that's farther from the opponent and then turning away from her is the most likely chance to escape. She keeps her elbows in tight—she doesn't want to give her opponent a chance to armbar her.

3. Butts continues to turn onto her stomach.

4. Once she gets to her stomach, she gets up on her knees to get back up. After that, she should turn to face her opponent and attack. We want to emphasize this: When practicing any escape, don't just practice getting out of a bad position; practice getting out of a bad position and attacking.

OUTSIDE-TURN ESCAPE: Variation

1. Ronda Rousey chooses an upper four-corner hold, and she starts as close as possible to the opponent. There isn't really an "outside" direction that Crystal Butts could use to turn away from Rousey. Butts is going to have to make a snap judgment. That is the purpose of this drill—to learn to make those judgments correctly. Regardless, she wants to put both her arms in front of her, bent at the elbows.

2. In Step 1, there is more space to Butts' left side. From this position on the bottom, she turns on her left shoulder and keeps her right arm between her body and Rousey's. The top player will usually grab under the armpit for the pin, but as Butts turns hard to the left, that grip is going to be ripped out. It's hard to hold back someone's whole body with one hand. Just like in the previous example, reaction time is important. Once Rousey has a tight grip and has settled her weight on Butts' chest, it is usually too late to escape.

3. At this point, Rousey is holding on with just her fingertips. Butts keeps turning in order to get to her knees and into a position to attack.

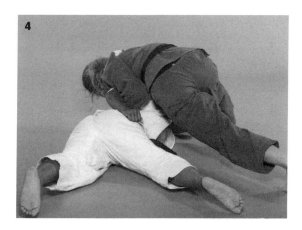

4. She keeps turning onto her stomach.

5. Butts backs up, away from Rousey, and gets onto her knees ...

6. ... and then attacks. We don't show a specific attack because there isn't one specific attack. This whole book is full of attacks on the mat. Take your pick. Again, the point of this drill is not just to escape but to win.

COACHING TIP:
LEARNING TO TURN IN THE RIGHT DIRECTION

In the pin-escape drill, both the bottom player's arms are bent and kept close to the body. If the bottom player had turned in the wrong direction or had overextended an arm, the opponent could lock the arm, throw a leg over and armbar.

After a few armbars, the defending player will learn to turn in the right direction and keep the arms in close to the body, and the attacking player will learn to watch for that arm-lock opportunity. Thus, this drill is one means of teaching a feel for armbars.

ARM-LOCK ESCAPE DRILLS

These next drills demonstrate what to do when you are already in the armbar, or arm lock. When a person is in an arm lock, it is common that one of two things will happen, both of them bad. Either the person panics and taps right away, fearful of getting a joint dislocated, or he or she tries to fight it and ends up injured. If you want to escape an arm lock safely, the time to figure out what to do is before you are in that position. The wrong thing to do, which is what many people do in this position, is try to lock both hands together and pull away from the opponent. As you turn away, if your opponent manages to break your grip, your arm is going to fly straight back as he or she leans back and arches. "Straight" is the worst possible word to have in a sentence that has "arm lock" in it.

After these 10-second escape drills, take 10 seconds and then switch positions. We usually go a few rounds back and forth and then switch partners. The main point of this drill is for the person on the bottom to learn to react quickly and correctly to escape. It is also good practice for the player on top in executing an armbar against resistance.

We'll say it again—this is a *drill*. Your whole goal in life, if you are the player on top, is to get out of that position without being armbarred. That being said, we have often found that our students have problems with arm-bar escape drills because they want more specific guidance than "Get the hell out of there!"

ARM-LOCK ESCAPE DRILL NO. 1: From the Bottom

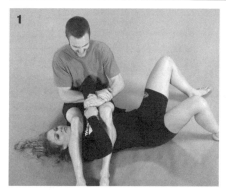

1. This arm-lock, or armbar, escape drill begins with a terrible position for Ronda Rousey, who is on the bottom. Travis McLaughlin has both his legs across her chest, knees pinched together and an arm locked against his body. She is seconds away from getting armbarred. When the coach yells "Go!" she has 10 seconds to escape.

2. Rousey needs to turn into the opponent and drive an elbow to the mat as hard and fast as possible. If she can get her elbow on the mat and keep it there, she can't be armbarred. McLaughlin, of course, is trying to pull off the armbar before Rousey can escape.

3. Rousey continues turning as hard and fast as she can into him.

4. She continues turning until she is completely out of the armbar.

5. Then she attacks. (Students should get in the habit of always being on the attack.)

HOW *NOT* TO ESCAPE AN ARMBAR

In judo, if you stand up and lift your opponent off the mat, the referee will stop the match, so you have escaped the armbar. Standing up is almost always the wrong choice to make when being armbarred.

Take a look again at the beginning of this drill. In this example, Travis McLaughlin has grabbed Ronda Rousey's forearm with both hands and has one leg on each side of her arm. She is not being armbarred because her arm is bent. If she stands up, the odds are very great she is going to end up straightening that arm and getting armbarred. If someone is trying to dislocate your elbow, the natural tendency is to get away; you have a better chance if you drive into the opponent than if you pull away.

ARM-LOCK ESCAPE DRILL NO. 1: If the Bottom Player Isn't Fast Enough

1. Crystal Butts starts on her back, and Ronda Rousey has her almost in an armbar.

2. Rousey leans back as fast as she can, keeps her legs together across Butts' body, arches her hips and completes the armbar.

ARM-LOCK ESCAPE DRILL NO. 2: From the Top

1. Ronda Rousey is on her knees, and Travis McLaughlin has her arm locked and his legs across her body. When the coach says "Go!" she has 10 seconds to escape.

2. To escape, she'll drive into her opponent and "stack" him, pushing him onto his back and folding his legs up on his chest. This part is really the key to the whole drill. She wants to stack him onto his back by driving into him, and he doesn't want to let her do that.

3. With McLaughlin stacked on his shoulder blades, she steps toward his head, driving his weight onto his shoulder blades and pulls her arm free. Once she has escaped, she follows up into an attack. (In mixed martial arts, the follow-up may be striking.)

Continued on next page

Alternative to Step 3

3a. Once Rousey has McLaughlin stacked on his shoulder blades, she has options: Judo players and grapplers may follow up into a pin. She grabs around both his legs and pulls up so he goes flat on his back.

3b. She reaches behind his neck with the hand nearest his head while still pulling his legs toward her with her far hand.

3c. She pulls her arms together so she is pulling his legs up to his chest.

TURNOVER DRILL: WRESTLER'S ROLL

In the first chapter, we mentioned that being on the bottom is not always a bad thing and gave the wrestler's roll as an example of what you can do from the bottom position. A wrestler's roll is a turnover done by the player on the bottom in mat work. Being on the bottom in a "turtle position" with your arms in is probably completely opposite of everything you have been taught. This is a bad position because you are exposing your back to the opponent, giving up all sorts of opportunities to be turned over, choked or arm-locked. It's also a great way to bait your opponent to enter into mat work. Also, sometimes you will get into this position to get out of an even worse position. (See Chapter 8.)

However you got there, whether your opponent knocked you down and forced you into this position or you were trying to sucker your opponent into mat work with you, the task is the same—to get off the bottom by rolling your opponent into a pin.

TURNOVER DRILL: Wrestler's Roll

1. When the instructor yells "Reach!" Crystal Butts is going to start her mat work from the position above, reaching to get a grip and turn over, choke or arm-lock any way she wants.

2. From the bottom position, Ronda Rousey reaches up and locks above the elbow on the farthest arm of the top player. (If the top player is reaching under her left side, then she is going to trap her left arm by hooking her left arm over it.)

Continued on next page

3. Rousey pulls in her right arm, giving the opponent little space to reach in to control the head for a choke. Now Butts has to think about defending as well as trying to pull off a technique of her own.

4. Rousey rolls toward the opponent, pushing off with her legs to drive her over. She shoves her right elbow back and uses it to help lift the opponent. Usually that elbow is going to end up lifting the far leg.

5. As Rousey rolls, Butts is going to land on her back, with Rousey on top.

6. She'll continue the roll, keeping the arm locked above the elbow. Her right arm is going to end up behind the opponent's head.

7. Rousey turns all the way through so that she is on her stomach. At this point, she is ready for blows to the body (in mixed martial arts).

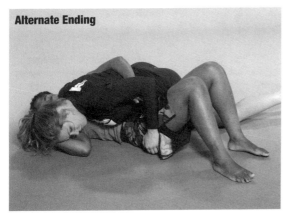

Alternate Ending

Alternate Ending For a pin in judo or grappling, Rousey turns all the way through so that she is on her stomach, one arm behind the opponent's head and the other arm locking her arm tight against her body.

HOW *NOT* TO DO A WRESTLER'S ROLL DRILL

It's important to note that this is a drill. At many clubs, players practice this technique and look very impressive, but they never actually pull off the move in a tournament because they don't drill it properly.

The wrong way to do this drill is for the player on the top to reach far over the bottom player's back.

They drill like this at some clubs—it is easy to get the roll and looks very nice in practice. Another mistake is to let the player on the bottom know when to expect the arm to be close, often going so far as to ask the partner, "Are you ready?"

This is a lousy imitation of competition, in which no one is going to lie across your back and reach an arm over so you can roll him or her over. The purpose of a drill is to practice for the exact situation you'll find yourself in during competition.

TURNOVER DRILL: How the Wrestler's Roll Could Go Wrong

1. Remember, this is a drill. We keep saying that over and over because we have found that far too often students cooperate and act as if these drills are no different than a series. The difference is this: If your opponent makes a mistake, you nail her. While your opponent is trying to escape from a disadvantageous position, you are trying not to let her. In this instance, if Ronda Rousey doesn't do the roll correctly, in particular, if she locks Crystal Butts' arm below the elbow, when she tries the roll ...

2. ... she cannot do it. She ends up underneath the opponent and gets pinned.

BASIC ARM LOCK TO PIN DRILLS

For the player on top, the purpose here is to practice a combination from pin to arm lock and back again. For the player on the bottom, it is an opportunity to practice escapes.

After Step 1, there are at least three different pins and two different armbars possible. The point of these drills is not for the player on top to do a specific pin or to get the armbar. The point is to win. For the player on the bottom, the goal is to escape. This is an opportunity for the player on the bottom to practice escapes from armbars as well as escapes from pins. For the player on top, it is an opportunity to practice breaking the arm free on a strong defensive player.

Having said that, we know how frustrated athletes get, especially if they are not very experienced, when they are not given some direction. Many athletes ask for more explanation when we just say, "You! On the top! Do the armbar, and if you can't get the armbar, do the pin! You! On the bottom! Don't let her do that!"

If you are one of those players who wants more detail, these drills include a few examples of what you might do. Keep in mind, though, that these are just examples and not the only options. In fact, neither of the techniques Rousey demonstrates are the one preferred by co-author De Mars. That's OK, though. If you try something else and get the pin or armbar, or if you escape from the bottom, then good for you. If it works, it's right.

> My last two years of competition, I dislocated a few people's arms. This isn't because I got meaner or even all that much better. As I got into higher levels of competition, people were less willing to give up, especially when an international medal was on the line.
>
> About the same time, I started to notice something really odd. The more I got a reputation for being "an arm breaker" the more people I pinned. It made sense when I thought about it. My opponents were focusing so much on fighting off being armbarred that they forgot to defend against being pinned.
>
> On the flip side of that, I have seen competitors who are so focused on executing an armbar that they completely miss opportunities for a pin that are right in front of them. A major problem these competitors have is that they don't have that "feel for the mat" simply because they don't do enough mat work. They haven't been in those positions often enough to develop the "spider sense" of knowing when to react. The basic arm lock to pin drill is one (of many) ways to develop that sense.
>
> —*AnnMaria De Mars*

BASIC ARM LOCK TO PIN DRILL

1. The drill begins with Crystal Butts on her back, arms locked together. Ronda Rousey, the player on top, puts her arm through the opponent's arm, hooked at the elbow.

2. It would be great if Rousey could lock the arm against her body, rotate toward Butts' head to rip the arm out, then pinch her knees tight, rotate back and apply the straight arm lock. That should be the first thing Rousey tries, and if she gets it, fine. She'll have worked on breaking the arm free, and her opponent will have learned a valuable lesson about being ready and holding on tighter. However, because the drill begins by letting the opponent (on the bottom) lock her hands together as tightly as possible, chances of pulling off an armbar right off the bat are not that great. Usually, the opponent holds on for dear life and neither person gets anywhere. Both are back where they started.

BASIC ARM LOCK TO PIN DRILL: Scenario No. 2

1. Ronda Rousey is in the position on top. Crystal Butts is just too strong, and Rousey can't get that arm out, so she switches to a pin. There are a few possibilities. However, she must remember that she has one arm looped through the opponent's arm pulling it toward her body. She never stops pulling that arm into her body.

2. Rousey grabs the opponent's legs on the outside and pulls them toward her.

3. One of Rousey's legs was across Butts' face; Rousey brings that leg behind her. The other leg hooks under the opponent's shoulder. She sits up into the pin. As she does this, her body is on her opponent's arm.

4. Rousey scoops Butts' hips toward herself with her right arm; her left arm is looped through the opponent's arms. She leans her weight forward. Butts is pinned.

Continued on next page

5. Rousey's leg is under her opponent's shoulders, so Butts doesn't succeed at turning away; she has to turn into Rousey. If Butts does that, Rousey throws her foot back across her face and does a push-up with her right arm, stretching out her body.

6. Rousey arches her back to do the push-up armbar.

7. If Step 6 doesn't work, she sits back for the straight armbar.

BASIC ARM LOCK TO PIN DRILL: Scenario No. 3

1. If she can't get the armbar, Ronda Rousey will go for a really tight pin. Her left arm is through Crystal Butts' right arm. She has both arms clasped tight together, and Rousey cannot break her grip. She has one leg across her face and the other leg across her body.

2. With her right hand, Rousey feeds the bottom of the jacket of Butts' gi into her hand.

3. Rousey grabs her opponent's far leg.

Continued on next page

4. She pulls Butts' legs to the side.

5. One of Rousey's legs was across Butts' face; Rousey moves that leg to step behind herself. She drives her body forward, with the leg that was across Butts' body hooking under her left shoulder.

6. Rousey leans forward into an "opponent sandwich." Her right leg is underneath Butts' shoulder, and all her bodyweight is on Butts' upper body. Her right arm is trapped by her own judo gi being wrapped around it and held in her left hand. Her right arm is holding Butts' legs to the side so she cannot push off from the mat to escape.

BASIC ARM LOCK TO PIN DRILL: Scenario No. 4

1. Crystal Butts is on her back with Ronda Rousey's left arm looped through her right arm. Rousey has one leg across Butts' face and the other leg across her body. Butts is holding on with both hands as tightly as she can, but she needs to get out of this position.

2. Rousey grabs the bottom of Butts' gi to feed it into her other hand.

3. The best chance of escape for Butts is to drive off with her feet and drive her elbow toward the mat. She should turn as hard and fast as she can toward the opponent.

COACHING TIP:
ADVANTAGES OF DRILLS

Drills offer several advantages. One is that they allow you to be in common positions and experiment with the best ways of getting out of a bad situation. As we always tell our athletes, the middle of a match is a bad time to have to come up with a plan. A second advantage is that drills allow advanced players to further develop their skills even when working out with players who are less experienced. Take the two athletes demonstrating these last few drills. Crystal Butts is lighter and younger than Ronda Rousey. It is a pretty safe bet that Rousey could armbar her 99 times out of 100. That doesn't help either of them get much better. By doing an armbar drill that requires Rousey to switch out of the armbar into a pin, she gets to practice switching positions for those times when she cannot catch a player with the first armbar, and Butts gets the opportunity to practice her escapes. Both players benefit. That is one of the major principles of judo—mutual benefit and welfare.

CHAPTER 8

SITUATION DRILLS

In many drills in this chapter, you'll notice that the techniques are not all technically perfect. There are three reasons for this:

1. We want to demonstrate mistakes your opponent might make and how you may take advantage of those mistakes.

2. We are showing you how to set up an opponent by deliberately doing an "incorrect" technique, to bait the opponent into a reaction.

3. We realize that, as a competitor, you are not perfect. Sometimes you will make a mistake, get an imperfect throw or get into a bad position. Maybe you are a beginner, training with other beginning competitors. Some books (and competitors and instructors) simply insist that everyone should always be perfect. There is no such thing as a right way to do things. If you win, it's right!

Before the world title fight between Tate and Rousey, Bas Rutten on the television show *Inside MMA* asked Tate to demonstrate how she was going to escape Rousey's armbar. Tate's answer was, "First of all, Bas, I'm not going to be in that position because I'm not going to let her throw me."

Although Tate's positive attitude was admirable, it doesn't seem to us a realistic basis for a training plan. Because Rousey did, in fact, throw Tate several times during the fight and then armbar her, all within five minutes, practicing reaction drills might have been a good idea.

There are two reasons that people lose—or miss an opportunity to win—on the ground. First, they only know a limited number of techniques on the ground. They have to move from the side of the opponent to in front because they don't have any moves they can do from the opponent's right side. There should be no position, no place on the mat, where your opponent is safe from you. We hope that the previous chapters helped with that aspect of your game.

Second, people miss winning opportunities—or, worse yet, get caught themselves—because they have not practiced moving from one position to another. Maybe you have a mat-work combination or two, a move you do to transition from a standing technique to mat work. If so, you are ahead of the game because most people don't have even that. The next step is to drill so much that when you find yourself in a situation, you react automatically.

The series in Chapter 4 all illustrate one method of winning on the ground. You begin with a plan that you follow through until winning is inevitable. That is one way to win, and it works for a lot of people. It teaches you a number of techniques that will work. Now we want to look at winning from a different angle. Transition drills are a second way of training to win on the ground. Don't misunderstand us. This isn't like a religion or voting for president. You don't have to pick one or the other. However, we have found that most people do have a preference. Some people like the structure of a mat-work series. Others find it boring and have a hard time forcing themselves to go through the same routine over and over.

There is a "perfect" way to do a technique. Here's how to do a perfect armbar, for example, if you have all the time you need and an opponent who is not resisting: Lock the arm against your body, pinch your knees together, hold the opponent's arm at the wrist and arch.

There are a couple of tiny problems, though. People resist when they are being armbarred—they resist a lot. You almost never have all the time you want. At most, you have a few seconds before the opponent turns over onto his or her stomach or pulls guard and gets out of position. In judo, you might get a few more seconds before the referee stands you up and makes you start again.

Situation drills are just as they sound, a way of training for the types of situations that are almost certain to happen in a competition. Transition drills are one type of situation drill. The point of a transition drill is to develop two or three options and practice them so often that you do them almost automatically. In other words, you will have practiced a few techniques so many times from a given situation that when it happens in competition, you will react automatically. Because of that, we sometimes also call them reaction drills.

Wait a minute, you say. There are dozens of possible situations: You're in his guard, he's in your guard, he's on all fours with you in front, you're on your elbows and knees with him at your side, you're ahead, he's ahead. Do we expect you to practice for all those situations?

Do they all occur in a match? Yes.

Well, then, yes—you should practice for all of them.

Ever notice how some people just know what to do when they hit the mat? It's because they practiced for that same situation before.

Here are the drills that can help you improve your score on the techniques test we gave you at the end of Chapter 1. We start with the simplest example of a transition drill, from a throw to a pin to an armbar. Next, we go to several drills that are all reactions to your opponent's actions.

The great advantage of all these drills is that you can practice them anywhere with anyone. If you get to practice and there is only one other person to train with and he or she is a beginner half your size, you can still work on developing your reaction time in common mat-work situations. Many clubs devote a half-hour or so of time at the beginning or end of practice when players can work on whatever skills they choose. That's a good time to run through some of these transition drills.

Transitioning from standing straight into mat work is a skill not many people practice, which is surprising because, in a real match, competitors somehow must switch from standing to ground work. Logically, you'd expect people to practice making that transition. When you watch most practices, whether judo, mixed martial arts or grappling, though, you will see the opposite. There will be drills and sparring standing up. Then the instructor announces it is time to do mat work, and everyone will get down on the mat and start fighting, already on the ground. It doesn't really make sense, does it?

The first drill we cover is so basic that we teach the first few steps of it even to 4- and 5-year-olds. We are trying to "drill" into them from the very beginning the idea of following up into mat work.

DRILL: One-Armed Shoulder Throw to Pin to Armbar

1. Ronda Rousey comes into a one-armed shoulder throw. Note where her right hand is holding. That hand is not going to move throughout this technique.

2. Travis McLaughlin blocks her so that she cannot complete the throw.

3. She drops on both knees and does a double-knee shoulder throw (seoi nage).

4. She completes the throw, still pulling up with that right hand and immediately goes into a pin.

5. Rousey spreads her legs out wider to give herself a more stable base to prevent McLaughlin from rolling her over his body.

6. She lets go of his arm with her left hand and grabs around his head for a scarf hold (kesa gatame) pin.

Note that her right hand is still in the same place as in Step 1. This is the key point in transition drills. She is making a smooth shift from standing to mat work and going right into the mat-work technique with the move she began with while standing. (To have a technically perfect scarf hold, she should have a grip on his left arm with her right hand and also have it trapped under her armpit. She doesn't want to do a picture-perfect hold down. In fact, she wants him to pull his arm away.)

7. If he tries to pull his arm away toward his head, she pushes the arm down.

Continued on next page

8. Rousey hooks McLaughlin at the wrist with her left leg.

9. She thrusts forward with her pelvis to apply the armbar.

10. Often, the opponent will pull out the arm that is trapped and pull toward the other player's back to escape the armbar. In this situation, Rousey hooks the arm at the wrist with her right leg.

11. She thrusts forward with her pelvis to complete the armbar.

REACTION DRILLS FOR TRANSITION FROM STANDING TO MAT WORK

In all these drills, both players are giving 90 percent. (We say 90 percent because it's not a contest. You want to look out for your teammate a little. If you go 100 percent in practice, what do you do in a contest?)

Here's a key point: In every one of these drills, both players should be attacking. That doesn't mean both players attack immediately, as the first drill demonstrates. In fact, the point of reaction drills is for both players to react (thus the name of these drills). One player makes a move, usually a throw, and then both players react to the position that results.

WHY WE DO THESE DRILLS

A famous comedian once said that the problem with women isn't that they leave you but that they have to tell you why. Well, here we are going to tell you why we do these drills, how this book almost got finished late and how I learned judo from a 13-year-old blue belt.

My Story About the Help 'Em Up Drills

Dr. Rhadi Ferguson and I were putting the finishing edits on our books. On Twitter, I challenged him to a race. Ferguson and I, being competitive types, were doing our best to win. Even though I started out 175 pages ahead of him, he almost beat me because this chapter is the one that Jim Pedro and I had the most disagreements on.

Pedro is a brilliant coach, no question about it. While I was writing this, he was working with the 2012 U.S. Judo Olympic team in London, and they were lucky to have him. He is too much of a gentleman to tell me flat out he thinks I am crazy, but he often says, "Well, that could happen, but it's very unlikely."

Actually, he is right and wrong. Although some of the situations and techniques that I show are unlikely for people competing at the Olympic level, they are very likely for less-experienced players. For the international-level athletes he works with, Pedro is absolutely correct.

However, the majority of the people who read this book are going to be young players, parents or coaches of young players, and adults who have been doing judo, grappling or mixed martial arts for only a few years, at most. Many of them will compete against people who make "beginner mistakes" because they are relative beginners.

He is right that elite players will seldom make the mistake, for example, of holding on to the opponent while getting up from the mat. However, even very good players make basic mistakes once in a great while. I've done it and I don't want to call anyone out by name, but I have seen amazing competitors hesitate at the wrong instant and get nailed with something really basic. In fact, Pedro and I were sitting side by side at a previous Olympics when a Cuban player went in for a basic body-drop throw *(tai otoshi)*, scored and went into the Olympic finals. Yes, they make each one of them very seldom, but there are a lot of possible mistakes. So if you practice 20 different situation drills for situations that occur 1 percent of the time, then sooner or later you will nail your opponent. What about all the other times? Well, those are all the other chapters in this book! Also, part of your job as a competitor is to "encourage" your opponent to make those mistakes so they will happen more often. (For an example of how to do that, look at Help 'Em Up Drill No. 2.)

Here is how the Help 'Em Up Drill came about.

Years ago, I was at a tournament in Barstow, California, watching the 13- and 14-year-old division because Ronda was in it. She was only a 12-year-old green belt, but I had put her into a couple of divisions to get more matches. A young blue-belt girl from the Barstow Judo Club was competing. In her first match, her opponent was on one knee, the girl came in and threw for an *ippon* and won the match. Ronda was her second match, and it was almost a repeat of the first one. Ronda was on one knee, coming up, and the other girl came in, threw her and got her in a pin. It was only a *waza ari* (half a point), and Ronda got out of the pin, mad enough to spit nails, turned the other girl over and won. On the way home, we had a conversation that went something like this.

"What do you think about that girl who threw you?"

"Mom, she wasn't that good, she just got lucky."

"Pumpkin, I watched her match before you and I thought she was lucky. Then I watched her do it to you, and you almost never get thrown. Then I watched her do it to the two people after you. No one gets that damn lucky. We're going to go home and practice that. I'm calling it the Help 'Em Up Drill."

A year later, in the finals of the Junior Nationals, she threw her big rival with that exact move we'd seen in Barstow. Now, you might ask, "So what, some purple-belt 13-year-old kid beat some other purple belt 14-year-old kid—who really cares?" The answer is, that kid cares. It was not the Olympics. It was just the biggest thing she had won up to that time, it was the first time she had beaten that girl by a full point and it was a huge deal to her. So maybe these drills won't help you win the Olympics. Although, as Jim Pedro says, it is possible but very unlikely. The possibility is far greater they will help you win the Tulsa Grappling Tournament, Freestyle Judo Championships or your third amateur MMA match. You know what? I'm totally OK with that.

—*AnnMaria De Mars*

HOW TO DO THE HELP 'EM UP DRILLS

In a Help 'Em Up Drill, one player begins in a very bad position. The first thing this player needs to do is get out of that position and then attack. There are four variations of this drill, but all have the same points in common:

- The drill begins with both players standing, both having a grip on the other player. This is how most grappling and judo competitions begin, so it only makes sense to start this way.

- Your partner goes down on a knee. Until this point, the players are co-operating. Your partner is going to let you get him or her to one knee.

- The second the partner's knee touches the mat, you are both trying to win.

- There is no "correct" technique to do from this point. This is very frustrating to some players. They want a prescription, like the mat-work series, for what they should do in each situation. Too bad. The point of these drills is for you to get into mat-work situations and figure it out for yourself. The correct reaction depends on what your opponent does. The more you put yourself in these situations, the better your "spider sense" of knowing where your opponent is going to go and what you should do in response. If your opponent ends up pinned, choked or armbarred, you did it right.

In any situation, make sure you follow through into mat work without hesitation. We cannot stress this enough. The whole point of these drills is for you to transition from standing to mat work automatically. It doesn't matter whether you do a pin or an armbar, or what throw you do. What does matter is that you have a seamless transition from mat work to standing. That is, your grip when you end is the same as it was when you began. You are going into the pin in the air while you are throwing your partner. If you're doing an armbar, you have a grip on the arm and one of your legs already across the body when your partner hits the mat. We have heard far too many players whine, "The referee didn't give me time to use my mat work. I could have beaten him." If you were in a pin or armbar as you hit the ground, the referee wouldn't even enter into the picture.

HELP 'EM UP NO. 1

You attempt a throw and knock your opponent to one knee. You are still standing and still have a grip. Start mat work from there. You have 10 seconds before the referee (coach) yells "break." At the end of 10 seconds, you switch positions. Note: For the player who is on one knee, this is a terrible position to be in against a knowledgeable fighter, and you should never try to do this. Good players won't be in this position very often, and they'll only stay in it for a second, so you want to develop the reflex to hit during that second of opportunity.

You can do a major outside sweep *(osoto gari)* when you are the standing player and you have a grip on the same side as your opponent's knee that is up. (For example, you have a left-handed grip and the other player's left knee is up.) Because your opponent is in a terrible defensive position, you don't need the world's most perfect technique to pull this one off.

HELP 'EM UP NO. 1: Left Grip, Left Knee

1. They begin from a standing position, with both players having the same grip. In this example, it is a left-handed grip.

2. Ronda Rousey comes into a throw, but it is not very successful. She only succeeds in knocking Travis McLaughlin to one knee. In this case, she is doing an inside leg sweep (ouchi gari). What throw she does is not important, as long as she ends up knocking the opponent to one knee, with the leg nearest her sleeve grip up off the mat—in this example, it is her opponent's left leg.

3. The second her opponent's knee touches the mat, she steps in deep toward him with her right leg. If McLaughlin tries to stand up, even better— she'll pull him up and toward the back-left corner (the same direction that she stepped).

4. She hooks the leg that is up (the knee off the mat) with her left leg. She does an outside sweep (osoto gari).

5. She follows up into the pin. A major point of all transition drills is to train the reflex of going straight from standing techniques into mat work with no hesitation. That's what we're trying to "drill" into your head.

6. Just like it isn't important what specific throw she does, the particular mat-work technique she does isn't important, either. It's easy to do a pin from here, but if the spirit moves her, she'll go ahead and armbar him afterward.

HELP 'EM UP NO. 2

This begins exactly the same as the first drill, with you attempting a throw and knocking your opponent to one knee. As in the first drill, you are standing with a grip. Again, you start your mat work as soon as the opponent's knee hits the mat. You have 10 seconds before the referee yells "break." At the end of 10 seconds, the two players switch positions.

In the first drill, Rousey has a grip on her opponent's left sleeve; his left leg is up and his right knee is on the ground. In drill No. 2, she has a grip on her opponent's left sleeve again; her opponent's right leg is up and her left knee is on the ground.

It doesn't matter which knee it is because, for the player who is on one knee, this is a terrible position to be in against a knowledgeable fighter. Good players won't get into this position very often, and they'll only stay in it for a second, so you want to develop the reflex to hit during that moment of opportunity. You practice this drill with the left knee up and the with the right knee up for the same reason that you practice throws when your opponent is moving backward and when he or she is moving forward—because both situations occur in a match.

If your opponent, the bottom player, makes the mistake of trying to get up without letting go, this is your chance to really bury him or her as you "help 'em up."

HELP 'EM UP NO. 2: Left Grip, Right Knee

1. As in the first drill, they begin from a standing position, with both players having the same type of sleeve and lapel grip. In this example, it is a left-handed grip.

2. Ronda Rousey attempts a throw that knocks Crystal Butts to the knee on the side where she has Butts' sleeve gripped. For a player with a left grip, as shown here, that is going to be the partner's left knee. Rousey happens to have done an outside foot sweep. It doesn't matter what throw she uses, as long as she knocks Butts to her knee.

3. Butts falls to one knee. This time, the leg on the same side as Rousey's lapel hand is up. In this example, it is the right leg.

4. Rousey does a sweeping hip throw (harai goshi). She steps backward in a circle with her right leg.

5. With her right hand, Rousey pulls Butts' left arm up and across her chest, pulls up on her right lapel and pushes with her left hand. Basically, her arms are turning like a steering wheel on a car. As she is rotating her entire body, her left leg sweeps on the outside of Butts' legs.

Continued on next page

6. She keeps turning, landing on her partner's upper body. She still has the same grip on her right arm she had when standing. She slides her other arm underneath Butts' head and secures the pin.

7. Rousey throws the other foot across Butts' body, pulling up on the left arm as she does. She sits down next to her opponent's shoulder, locking the arm straight against her body, and arches her hips to apply the armbar. Although it is broken down step by step, when they are doing this drill, Step 5 through Step 7 should take half a second.

Alternate Step 6

Alternate Step 6 Rousey may decide to go from the throw (in Step 5) to an armbar. If Rousey stays standing, she'll end with her foot on one side of the opponent's head. Rousey still has the same grip on her opponent's right arm that she had when the opponent was standing.

COACHING TIP: DRILL WITH A PURPOSE

The difference between these drills and the mat-work series shown in Chapter 4 is that they are not scripted. That is, neither you nor your opponent knows exactly where you are going to end up. Often, you would do an inner-thigh throw *(uchi mata)* when your opponent, who is down, has the leg up on the opposite side from your sleeve grip—in this case, the right leg up. Yet Rousey did a *harai goshi* in Step 4 of drill No. 2. When asked why, she said, "Because I could *feel* her weight more on the left leg. I could *feel* her going that way."

We added the emphasis in that sentence because that is the whole entire point of this drill—to get a feel for the transition from an opponent down on one knee to a throw to mat work.

COACHING TIP: MAT WORK AS A COUNTER TO STANDING

In the first and second drills, you start the mat work by knocking your opponent down. Although the third and fourth drills are similar to the first two, except for the way the opponent gets to the mat, we encourage you to do these also. Why? Because most people don't automatically think of mat work as a counter to a standing technique.

HELP 'EM UP NO. 3

You begin this drill standing, with a sleeve and lapel grip. Your partner does a throw, misses and lands with one knee down on the same side as the sleeve you are holding. You are still standing with a grip on his sleeve. So if you have a grip on your partner's left sleeve, his left knee will be on the mat. Start your mat work from there. You have 10 seconds before the referee yells "break."

HELP 'EM UP NO. 3: Left Grip, Left Knee

1. The players are standing, both with a grip on the lapel and sleeve. At the risk of being repetitive, we keep saying that there is not a specific move as a goal but rather developing your own "mat-work sense." Here is a perfect example of how this drill can work.

2. When Travis McLaughlin comes in to do a throw, Ronda Rousey steps back and yanks down so that he misses and lands on both knees. Feeling himself being pulled down, he holds on to his grip and starts to stand up.

3. We show this from another angle to demonstrate why a player should never keep his grip while trying to stand back up. As he tries to do so, Rousey is in an even better position to pull him up. (This is why it's called "help 'em up.") She is applying one of the basic principles of judo—using her opponent's own force against him.

4. Rousey turns her body while pulling up on McLaughlin's left arm with her right hand and pulling up on his lapel with her left hand. She sweeps his leg on the outside.

5. She follows him to the mat as she throws.

6. Then she follows up into the pin. The arm that was on his lapel goes around his head. She still has the same grip on his left arm she had when she started the drill standing. A major point of all transition drills is to train that reflex of going straight from standing techniques into mat work with no hesitation. That's what we're trying to "drill" into your head.

HELP 'EM UP NO. 3: Alternate Ending

1. Here is drill No. 3 with a different result. It begins with both players standing.

2. Travis McLaughlin moves in to an outside leg sweep.

3. He misses.

4. Ronda Rousey hops forward on her right foot while sweeping upward with her left leg. She pulls his left hand across her body. With her right hand, she pulls his lapel up in the direction she is throwing, which is toward his left rear corner.

5. As she throws, Rousey continues straight to the ground.

6. Her legs split to give her a broad base. Her arm that was on his lapel slides around his neck. Notice that the grip she has on his sleeve is still in the same place as it was when she was standing up.

COACHING TIP:
DEVELOPING A FEEL

An outside leg sweep, as shown in Help 'Em Up Drill No. 1, is usually the best move when the standing player has a grip on the same side as the knee that is up (for example, a left-handed grip and the player has the left knee up). So why did Rousey do a different throw in Help 'Em Up Drill No. 3? Why did she attack the opposite leg?

Rousey said, "Because as he was coming up, I could feel his weight coming forward, so it only made sense to do a forward throw in that situation."

And that demonstrates the point of drills—developing that feel for when you should do a certain technique and then reacting to that feeling. The typical practice doesn't provide enough opportunities in which you are in a situation when moving from standing to mat work to get that "feel," so you want to use these drills to make that opportunity.

HELP 'EM UP NO. 4

You begin this drill standing, with a sleeve and lapel grip. Your partner does a throw, misses and lands with one knee down, and the knee that is on the same side as your lapel grip is up. So if you have a grip on his left sleeve and right lapel, his right knee will be up. You are still standing with a grip. Start your mat work from there. You have 10 seconds before the referee yells "break."

If you have a left grip and the person who is down has the other leg up—in this case, the right leg up—an inner thigh throw *(uchimata)* can be a really powerful move. If your opponent, the bottom player, makes the even bigger mistake of trying to get up without letting go, this is your chance to really bury him or her as you "help 'em up."

HELP 'EM UP NO. 4: Left Grip, Right Knee

1. Both players are standing, with a grip on the lapel and sleeve.

2. When Travis McLaughlin comes in to attack, Ronda Rousey steps out of the way so that he lands on his left knee, with his right knee up off the mat.

3. She pulls the opponent's left arm up and across her chest and pulls up on his right lapel with her right hand. Basically, her arms are turning like a steering wheel on a car. At the same time, her left leg goes between his legs, lifting at the inner thigh, while she rotates her entire body. Although she is an experienced judo player, neither Rousey's left arm nor her body are in the perfect position for this throw. It doesn't matter. If she catches him as he comes up, his own momentum will help her.

4. When she completes the throw, her left arm is in the perfect position to go into the pin. As she throws, that right arm should be going around the opponent's head.

5. She follows through into the pin. As she lands, her arm is already snaking around the opponent's neck. All she needs to do is split her legs apart and she has a scarf hold. (These drills benefit not just the player standing but also the player who is down. It won't take too many repetitions of this drill to break the habit of holding on to the gi and trying to stand up again. It is a terrible mistake, and we want to beat it out of you.)

COACHING TIP: WATCH FOR OPPORTUNITIES

Let us emphasize something about the first five drills. They all start the second that one player touches the mat with any part other than his feet. That means the person who is down almost always has a grip on the other's gi and vice versa. Any decent player is not going to stay in that position for more than a second or two because it is very disadvantageous. That second is your opportunity to attack.

Your success depends on catching that opportunity. Blogger and longtime judo practitioner Chad Morrison made the astute comment on my blog that being faster than your opponent doesn't necessarily rely on you being naturally a better athlete. Someone who practices these drills a thousand times is almost certain to react faster.

—*AnnMaria De Mars*

COUNTERING A THROW

As we've said (about 11 times), a good player is not going to stay in that position with a grip on your gi for very long. So what then? Well, read on.

The next set of drills also starts with the players standing, but these apply when you miss that first opportunity. From the standing position, your opponent attacks or you attack him or her. This time, your opponent is a lot smarter and the second he or she is on the mat, the player lets you attack and tries to drop into a defensive position. As with the last two drills, the next two are a reaction when your opponent tries to throw you. They involve chokes. Not too many people practice chokes as a counter to throws. Maybe that's why they work so often.

There are numerous possibilities for countering a throw. We cover a few of them here, both for the player standing and for the player on the bottom. The key point is that you should have two or three techniques and drill them religiously. Having two or three moves you have practiced so often that you react instinctively is far better than knowing a dozen techniques fairly well.

In most of these drills, we begin with the players standing because that is what you are practicing: the transition from standing to mat work, and yet we have found that most people don't do it. They not only don't normally do it, but they also don't even do it when we have them practice transition drills. They will start standing the first time, and for the next drill, they will start on all fours on the mat, which kind of defeats the purpose of a transition drill. Old habits are hard to break, and most people are in the habit of starting mat work with both players on the ground. As coaches, we need to keep reminding them to start standing, and that is why we are reminding you, as well.

COUNTERING A SHOULDER THROW: British Strangle Variation No. 1

1. In this drill, the situation is another common transition to mat work. This one also starts with both players standing and having a grip on each other. In this case, Travis McLaughlin only has one hand on Ronda Rousey because he is going to do a one-armed shoulder throw (ippon seoi nage).

2. He attacks, misses the throw and ends up on his knees. This happens either because the attacker tried a double-knee shoulder throw or because the opponent steps out of the way and pushes the attacker to the ground. The players have 30 seconds from this position to get a score. Both players should be attacking.

3. Rousey's first move is to step out of the way of the throw. If she stays in the position in which the attacker is in front of her and rolls over the player, a judo referee may count that as a continuation of the throw and give a score to the other player. Even in mixed martial arts, in which the throws don't really score in the same way as in judo, staying behind the bottom player opens an opportunity for him or her to pop up again on the shoulder throw and roll the opponent into a worse position. Take our advice: Step to the side, as Rousey does here. Once the top player has sidestepped the throw, there are many possibilities for an attack. One of our favorites is to do a rolling choke.

Not stopping the throw and sidestepping is the most common mistake players make. Then they get countered. You don't want that. Keep your right hand in the exact same position it was in when the two of you were standing and you had a right grip on the other player's lapel. That hand is never going to move. Keep that grip. As you step to the side, shove the opponent's left shoulder toward the mat, putting your weight on him. (Notice where Rousey's hand is in Step 3: It is on McLaughlin's left shoulder—it is not there to give him a friendly pat on the back.)

Continued on next page

4. When she sidesteps and pushes her opponent down, Rousey not only stops the throw but also loops McLaughlin's judo gi under his neck. Now she throws her leg over.

5. Her foot goes all the way across his body to the other side and she rolls under him.

6. She uses the leg that is across his body to roll him onto his back while grabbing at the bottom of the leg nearest to her.

7. Rousey keeps pulling throughout this move with her right hand under McLaughlin's neck. Her right leg is over his right arm to keep him from pulling the gi down, her left leg is across his body and her left hand is holding his leg at the ankle. He really has no option other than to lie there and be choked.

IMPORTANT POINT:
IT'S A DIVE, NOT A ROLL

In judo class, there was a game we used to play when we were children that illustrated this perfectly. It is also strongly discouraged by all judo organizations because it is dangerous. It went like this. One person would go down on his or her hands and knees and then we would do a forward roll over the person. After the whole line of kids did that, we'd have a second person kneel next to the first kid and the rest would do a rolling fall over both people. If you chickened out or if you missed and ended up falling on the second person, you were out. We kept adding people on the ground until only one person was left to do the roll. Instructors don't teach this drill because it is dangerous, and we don't recommend it. Just imagine the motion with your body if you were to dive over two or three people and do a rolling breakfall.

The drill helped us learn a diving breakfall, stretching the body out and then rolling back like a regular fall. The momentum carries you over and brings your opponent with you.

Another important point is that even with the momentum, if your opponent is much heavier, this will not work. Say I weigh 123 pounds (56 kilograms) and my opponent weighs 220 pounds (100 kilograms). I'd probably be able to get him or her somewhat off-balance, but I doubt I would be able pull the person all the way over. This technique works fine for competition by weight division because against a player of equal weight, with the momentum added by the diving motion, you can always pull him or her over and up. There is actually an equation that explains this:

Kinetic energy = ½ mass times velocity squared

This is why the diving part is so important. The more you can increase your velocity by diving outward, because this value is squared, the greater impact on total force applied to pull the opponent over.

—*AnnMaria De Mars*

COUNTERING A SHOULDER THROW: British Strangle Variation No. 2

1. As before, the players start from a standing position.

2. When Crystal Butts comes into the throw, Ronda Rousey blocks it.

3. She then steps around to the side so Butts cannot complete the throw.

4. If Butts had tried to come up, Rousey would do one of the Help 'Em Up drills, but she is smarter than that. Butts lets go and drops to her hands and knees.

5. To do the choke, Rousey dives toward her opponent's hips at a 45-degree angle. She does not dive straight over or she will end up underneath her opponent, get pinned and look stupid. She is doing a judo roll, a rolling breakfall. As she does it, she keeps her right hand on the lapel, exactly where it would have been from the beginning. We've said it before and we're saying it again: This hand never moves.

6. As she dives over the opponent, Rousey's left hand goes under the opponent's arm and behind her head.

7. Rousey's left hand goes under Butts' left arm and behind her head as she is diving over, not after she has completed the roll.

8. Rousey sits up into the choke in the position shown as she completes the roll. Her right hand holds the lapel that is now pulled tight under her opponent's neck. Rousey's left hand is under Butts' arm and is moving behind her head.

Continued on next page

9. When doing the usual rolling fall in judo, Rousey would come up to her feet. Here, instead of standing up, she sits up, choking Butts, as shown. But Rousey is not done yet.

10. From the sitting position, Rousey slides back on to her stomach. At this point, she chokes Butts and executes a pin.

11. To make the pin tighter, at the first opportunity, Rousey overhooks Butts' left arm with her left arm. In judo, this is called a single wing choke (kata hajime). Rousey keeps pulling with her right hand to continue the choke. Butts cannot move to her right without being choked and can't move to her left because Rousey has her arm trapped and her entire upper body in the way. All Butts can do is lie there and be choked.

COUNTERING A SHOULDER THROW: British Strangle Variation No. 3

1. As before, the players start from a standing position. Because Crystal Butts is doing a one-armed shoulder throw, she may only have a one-handed grip (and each player may hold the other's sleeve).

2. When Butts comes into the throw, Ronda Rousey blocks it, using her free hand on the opponent's shoulder to shove her face-first toward the mat.

3. Butts lets go of her grip to keep her face from hitting the mat. She ends up on her hands and knees, as shown. A smart, experienced player like Butts will automatically have her arms bent to make it difficult for Rousey to armbar her. Rousey makes it very clear to the referee that she stopped the throw. (Many times in tournaments the blue player in this situation would go around behind the white player to apply the choke. The player in white continues the throw. The player in blue gets thrown and has only himself or herself to blame.) Notice that just like in the previous technique, Rousey is standing and has her right hand on the opponent's lapel. This hand does not move.

Continued on next page

4

5

4. The next few steps happen in one or two seconds. Rousey moves to her opponent's side.

5. Rousey pulls up with her right hand (to make it difficult for Butts to flatten out) and slides her left hand under Butts' left arm. At the same time, Rousey throws her left leg across the opponent's back and around her stomach.

6

7

6. Rousey rolls hard to her left side. As mentioned in the previous technique, this is a move in which momentum carries the player through the roll and her opponent along with her.

7. As she rolls, Rousey drives her leg across Butts' stomach and her arm up behind her head. She does not wait until she has rolled over to try to slide that arm behind the opponent's head. This photo demonstrates the end of the roll. If Butts turns in, that would allow Rousey to slide her arm farther behind her head and choke her even better. If Butts turns out, that is going to pull the lapel hand tighter and the result, again, would be an even better choke.

COACHING TIP: PRACTICE ALTERNATIVES

When doing drills starting from a particular position, do the same couple of moves over and over. Don't have 67 different moves. Have a plan A and a plan B, each of which you practice 1,000 times a year. Then have a plan C and a plan D that you practice 500 times a year—each. If you do these so often, when you are in a particular position on the mat, you are going to hit that move, say, the choke as shown, automatically, without thinking. If for some reason you cannot get it—for example, if the other player turtles up too quickly and you cannot get the roll in fast enough—then you are going to go to Variation No. 3, automatically.

COACHING TIP: VARIATIONS

Of the variations of the technique commonly called the British strangle, Jim Pedro Sr. prefers the first one, the more standard British strangle, because it ends in a tighter choke. I prefer the second variation because it offers a natural transition to a pin. Ronda Rousey prefers the third variation in which she throws her leg through and has the opponent controlled between her legs at all times. No matter how many times Rousey tried it when she was young, she just did not feel comfortable with the diving roll across the opponent's body. This illustrates an important lesson. The point of judo isn't to slavishly imitate your instructor or your favorite world champion. The point is to win. If in doing a drill, like the standing transition drill, you find that certain techniques don't work, discard those and try something that feels more natural.

—AnnMaria De Mars

DRILLS FOR WHEN YOU ARE DOWN ON HANDS AND KNEES

This is actually the same as the previous drills but from the other player's perspective. Remember, in a drill, both people should be attacking. What if you are the player on one knee? Remember, these drills should benefit both players and both players should be attacking. If you are in this position, the absolute worst thing you can do is stand up quickly. View the pictures at the beginning of this chapter to see what happens.

If you are the player in blue, let go. Drop to all fours or go into "the guard," that is, sit on your butt, back off the mat, hands in front of you. If you get in this position, get out of it as quickly as possible and get into a more defensible position.

THE PLAYER ON ONE KNEE

This is a drill in which you try things to determine what works best for you. Some people would say that the correct move for the player on one knee is to let go and transition into the guard. Those same people might say that it is always a mistake to give up your back. It also may turn out to be a mistake to try to switch to the guard position because as you make the switch, the opponent runs you down, as demonstrated in the first Help 'Em Up Drill. Your first step is to make sure your opponent doesn't have a good grip on you when you hit the mat.

One possibility is to turtle up—completely opposite of everything you have probably been taught. This is a bad position because you are exposing your back to the opponent, giving up all sorts of opportunities to be turned over, choked or arm-locked. However, it is not nearly as bad a position as trying to stand up from one knee and getting slammed into the mat. If you do drop to all fours, you are still in a bad position.

Don't give your opponent a chance to try a choke or turnover. As soon as you are down on all fours, reach up, locking above the opponent's elbow with your right arm. Use your left elbow to lift him or her. Imagine the move you would make if you elbowed someone behind you in the face—not that you would ever do that.

You roll hard to your opponent's right, helping your opponent roll over by lifting with your left elbow, keeping the player's arm still locked under your right arm. Roll on top of him or her. Turn onto your stomach. The opponent's right arm should still be locked under your right arm. Reach your left arm up under the player's head. Grab his or her left arm with your right, turning completely onto your stomach for a side mount (yoko shiho gatame).

THE PLAYER ON ONE KNEE

1. Ronda Rousey's arm is inside her opponent's grip. Crystal Butts does not have a very good grip on the lapel, so when Rousey hits the mat on all fours, she ends up ripping out of her opponent's grip.

2. Rousey turtles up, dropping to all fours.

3. As soon as she is down on all fours, Rousey reaches up with her right arm, locking Butts above her elbow. She uses her left elbow to lift Butts.

Continued on next page

4. Rousey rolls hard to her right.

5. She helps roll the opponent over by lifting with her left elbow, keeping the opponent's arm still locked under her right arm.

6. Rousey rolls on top of Butts.

7. Rousey turns onto her stomach. The opponent's right arm is still locked under her right arm. Rousey reaches her left arm up.

8. She puts it under Butts' head. Rousey grabs Butts' left arm with her right, turning completely onto her stomach for a side mount.

COACHING TIP:
SETTING BAIT

Why would you drop into a position like this when you are clearly at a disadvantage? Why would you "give up your back" when so many instructors tell you not to do exactly that?

Let us pose a different question. Some athletes develop a reputation for being mat-work specialists. Every time they win a match, it is on the ground. So why do people keep going to the mat with them? Surely all their competitors are not stupid. It must occur to some of them not to go to the mat with a player known for winning on the ground. All the competitors' coaches can't be so clueless that they haven't noticed the person their athlete is going to fight wins almost all his or her matches on the ground. At least some of their coaches must have instructed the players, "Don't go to the ground! Keep the match standing!" So why do players go to the mat with

these people time and time again? How do they keep winning on the ground?

The question isn't, "How do they win on the ground?" It is, "How do they get their opponents on the ground in the first place?" One answer is the transition drills we described at the beginning of this chapter—they go into mat work as they are going to the ground, giving the opponent no chance to escape.

A second answer is that they "set bait" by putting themselves in a position that looks to be a disadvantage. In the heat of the moment, it is the exceptional opponent who can resist attacking.

If your opponent is noted for being very skilled on the mat and willingly gets into a disadvantageous position, there are a couple of possibilities: A) You are so great and intimidating that it has made your opponent forget all the mat work he or she ever learned or B) your opponent is setting you up.

Perhaps you really are that scary good but, personally, we think that "B" is more likely.

DEFENSIVE DRILLS

If you are ahead on points, defending on the mat can win the match for you. This is especially true in judo, in which the rules and scoring tend to favor standing technique.

The following defensive drills can be done from a variety of positions. The result is seven different situation drills. The players can start in the following positions:

1. face-to-face on their knees

2. in a referee's position from wrestling, with the attacking player on top

3. in a referee's position, with the attacking player on the bottom

4. with the defending player on his or her back in the guard

5. with the attacking player on his or her back in the guard

6. with the defending player on his or her stomach

7. with the attacking player on his or her stomach

DEFENSIVE DRILL: Eat Up the Clock

Here is a question we ask judo students: You are ahead on points and in this position on the mat. There are 30 seconds left on the clock. What do you need to do to win?

The answer is the same no matter what the position is: Simply, do not lose—do not get thrown, choked, pinned, armbarred or two penalties after the referee stands you up. There is no stalling penalty on the mat. Stay on the mat and eat up the clock, and then you are the winner. Of course, if you just fall flat to your stomach and don't do anything, the referee is going to stand you up. The point of the drill is to attack your opponent without taking any chances. If the opponent is attacking you, you want to defend enough to keep from losing the match, again, without taking any chances.

This drill works for defense and offense. If you are one of the stronger players in your club, you should be the person who is "losing" most of the times that you do this drill. It will give the weaker players a chance to "win" if they can hold you off, and it will make you better prepared for when you are in the situation when your opponent is just trying to eat up the clock.

DEFENSIVE DRILL: Get Off the Mat

Here is the situation: You are in a match with someone so much better on the mat than you that if you spend 30 seconds down there, that opponent *will* beat you. Your whole goal at this point is simple: Get off the mat. Don't be a hero, just stand up anyway you can and fight on your turf. Some people will say this is running away. We disagree. It is simply being smart and fighting on the terms that are most in your favor.

This is a good drill for the attacker and the defender. If you are a competitor who is really good on the mat, people will do anything to avoid being there with you. We have seen people get up from the ground and literally run away from the opponent because they were so scared. In this drill, if the player who is supposed to get up manages to stand, the other player loses. Again, this is a good drill if you have players who are somewhat mismatched because it gives one player, who could perhaps never beat the other on the mat, a chance to "win." It also forces the player who could normally win in mat work to work harder.

CHAPTER 9

ESSENTIALS OF WINNING ON THE GROUND

This book is all about winning. That isn't to say that there is never more to martial arts or sports than who wins a match. Of course, everyone knows that is not true. You learn discipline. You test yourself in ways that people who spend their entire lives behind a desk can only imagine. Sports and martial arts can teach you a lot about life.

WINNING DOES MATTER

Winning has been a big part of our lives and of those we have taught and coached. It's popular to say that it doesn't matter whether you win or lose and that it's the journey, not the destination, and all those other things people say in those leagues where every person gets a medal. It's popular to say, but it would be lying to tell you that winning doesn't matter. It matters to us, and we believe that it matters to most people. There's no substitute for competition, and there is nothing like winning.

When you stand on the podium and see your country's flag go up in the stadium and hear your country's anthem being played, and know that it's playing because of you—there is no other feeling like it on earth.

The first time your little son or daughter goes out on the mat and pulls off that move you have been working on and wins a match—there's nothing like that, either.

When you beat that person who you have fought two or three times before, and lost, and this time you win—it's a great feeling!

You learn so many things from competition, when you step onto the mat, step into the cage, face your fears and refuse to back down. This isn't a philosophy book, though, so we'll just leave it at this—winning on the ground is a sign of hard work, discipline, focus and training.

Our aim in writing this book was to teach you some techniques and drills that will improve your chances of winning using mat work. As teachers, we want each and every one of our students to get better. When you can beat people you couldn't beat before, doing techniques you've pulled off in competition for the first time, that's a sign you're getting better.

WINNING IS DIFFERENT FOR EVERYONE

Each person is different and will grasp things at different times. When you learn some techniques, it may take you a lot longer than other students.

Other moves may come easy to you. With enough hard work and repetition, you should be able to pull off anything covered in this book. Be patient and don't give up when it seems difficult.

We have looked at mat work from different points of view. We have covered very precise series that are very methodical, step by step. We have discussed quick reactions to opponents' mistakes that end in armbars or pins.

Some of the techniques—those that rely on gripping the gi—will only work in judo or jiu-jitsu. Most of those moves, though, can be changed slightly by grabbing the head, arm or wrist and work just as well in grappling or mixed martial arts. We encourage you to experiment, to change these techniques, drills and combinations to fit you.

One reason we've been attracted to martial arts/combat sports our whole lives is the freedom that they offer. It's not like swimming, in which you have to do a particular stroke the exact same way as everyone else, and if you don't, you're disqualified. We believe in teaching a lot of different techniques and allowing individuals to work on the techniques that come easy to them so they can practice what is right for their body types, their athleticism, their personality. Although we have tried to emphasize which are the traditional or "correct" ways of doing a particular move—the ways that most people do a technique—we've also showed variations.

It's not the purpose of this book, nor of our teaching on the mat, to make athletes who are little clones of us, doing the same things or doing the style of mat work we do unless it fits them personally. If you win, it's right.

THE ODDS ARE IN YOUR FAVOR IF YOU KNOW HOW TO WIN ON THE GROUND

Having just said that one size doesn't fit all, we don't want to leave you with the wrong idea that every way you might train or compete is just as likely to win as anything else. Maybe you'll enter a match, lie flat on your back and let the opponent get on top of you. Gerda Winklbauer (1980 World Judo lightweight champion) actually won some matches that way, slipping in a choke as the opponent tried to pass the guard. So, yeah, lying on your back might work, but we wouldn't bet on it.

There are really four keys to winning on the ground. The first is to be strong in the areas in which most people are weak. For judo and mixed martial arts, this is ground work as a whole. In general, people tend to prefer to fight standing, so if you are good on the ground, you'll find it easier to win matches. The competition is less there.

In judo and mixed martial arts, you see very few mat-work combinations or counters. In grappling and jiu-jitsu, which have scoring systems that allow much more time on the ground, you see a lot of attempted counters and combinations, but you also see a relatively slower pace than in judo or mixed martial arts. You don't see quick reactions on the mat as often as you do with the best judo players and mixed martial artists.

The second key is discipline. You don't need to practice every technique in this book a thousand times. What you do need is to select a few that fit you personally and then do each of those 10,000 times. Does that sound impossible? Do 50 repetitions a day, and you'll have done 18,250 in a year. It's actual math. It shouldn't take you an hour to do 50 repetitions, either. It will if you stop between each one and talk about the movie you saw last week, your girlfriend or how it's too hot in the gym. You ought to be trying to increase your speed on your mat techniques, anyway.

When you first get started, it might take you and a partner 25 minutes to each run through 50 repetitions. Come to practice 25 minutes early and leave 25 minutes late. As you practice more, you'll find you can get through your repetitions in 20 minutes and then 10 or 15. If your club is like most, you won't find someone else as dedicated as you, so you'll end up working with one person before practice and a second person after practice. The beauty of the series, combination and counters we have included is that you will benefit from doing the repetitions on anyone. You don't need someone your same size, strength or skill level. Anybody will do.

You do need to take practice seriously. This doesn't mean beating up on your partner, but it does mean doing your repetitions as fast as you can, with little rest time in between. Running through these moves quickly will get you in better condition. Also, the less time you spend during practice resting or socializing the more repetitions you can get in.

The third key is physical conditioning. Although it's true that technique will beat strength, technique plus strength will beat technique alone. The more you train the better and stronger you will get, and there is nothing better for training in mat work than doing mat work. Of course, in the United States and Canada, it's often difficult to get in enough hours of practice (and it's less in some other countries) each day to be in top shape. Conditioning for judo, grappling and mixed martial arts is a big topic and could be an entire book in itself. Although it has not been the focus of this book, just be aware that your physical strength and conditioning are important. Maybe that will be our next book.

The fourth key is mental. Your opponent can have better technique, more physical strength, but if you are determined enough, if you refuse to give up and keep attacking, keep fighting, sometimes you can pull out the win. On the flip side, we have seen people who had the ability to win but who just lacked confidence or mental strength. Under pressure, they would panic, make mistakes and let a weaker, less-skilled opponent beat them.

Now, if we had the true secret to mental conditioning, we probably wouldn't be writing a book on mat work. Well, we might still be writing this book, but we'd be writing it from our houses on our private islands that we bought with the billions of dollars we made from selling the secret to mental strength. We can tell you this: A part of confidence comes from knowing that you are prepared. If you can look across at your opponent and truly tell yourself, "There is no way he trained harder than me," then you are a long way toward having the mental strength to win. Part of that refusal to lose comes from having sacrificed so much and trained so hard that you are just determined to make it all worthwhile.

WHAT IT TAKES TO WIN

Perhaps professional mixed-martial artist and judo black-belt Roman Mitichyan summed it up best. He had just come back from the 2002 World Sambo Championships where he won a bronze medal. He said to De Mars, "You know, when I was a kid, there were a lot of guys in the *dojo* who were better than me. Then they would start missing practice, say, one Friday a month, to go out with a girl or study for an exam. I went to every practice and got better. Then they were missing every Friday, and I was still going to every practice. So I started winning against all those guys. Now, here I am with a medal from the World Championships and where are they? Sitting on a couch somewhere, fat and out of shape."

No one wins every match, but if you follow the drills and techniques in this book, you'll win more. The more you train—particularly the more you train in the right way, on the skills that are most likely to be successful in competition—the more you will win. We can't promise you will always win, but we can guarantee that if you apply the lessons from this book regularly, you will get better. In the end, that is what winning means, that in that match, you were the better person and that is why ...

victory is sweet.

APPENDIX

THE LION, THE ANACONDA AND REACTION DRILLS

The first lesson you need to learn in coaching is that not every student is like you.

Bear with me as you read the following story. There is a point here. I promise.

Imagine you are an anaconda, lying in the grass, digesting the deer you caught a week ago, when a pride of lions comes by. You and the head lion get into a discussion about hunting. He explains his method of hunting to you. It is very organized. The lions stalk a herd of deer, following a scent. They select a deer that is slower than the others. They chase the herd one way and then the other until this deer is separated. They chase it down until it is exhausted. One lion leaps at the back legs and cuts the hamstrings. Another lion goes for the neck, and the result is deer meat for dinner.

The lion asks the anaconda, "So how do you hunt?"

You reply, "Well, I just lay here in the grass, and when something comes by, I wrap around it, squeeze it to death and swallow it whole."

The lion exclaims, "That's wrong! That's not how you do it! How often does something just walk right by you? Maybe you'd catch something really slow and sick that way, but no, you have to chase things down and kill them. That's what hunting is. Besides, look at you. You can't swallow a deer whole. That is impossible. I don't mean to call you a liar, but it sounds pretty unlikely to me."

Now you are confused. On the one hand, you've seen the lions hunting and they *are* the king of beasts. You have to admit that they look really impressive and beautiful chasing deer in a disciplined formation across the plains. It certainly *sounds* like the Lion King is right. He is, after all, a lion.

On the other hand, you're lying there digesting a deer you've caught and you're a 30-foot-long, 500-pound anaconda, the largest snake in the world, which means you've actually caught a whole lot of deer. It's all very confusing.

The lion is equally troubled by the thought of the anaconda spreading this misinformation on hunting to little snakes. Why, they'll surely starve to death except for the odd exceptionally lucky one here and there.

This is almost exactly the conversation Jim Pedro Sr. and I had one day. Well, it would have been if Jim were a lion and I were a giant snake and we were talking about judo instead of hunting.

I'd say that about two-thirds of the time that I sent him anything for this book, he'd call me up and say, "That's wrong. You did that wrong. It won't work."

I listened to him because I have a lot of respect for his judo knowledge, but at the same time, I would think, "I know it works because I did it lots of times and not just on little kids but at the world level. I even do it sometimes now on people way younger and stronger than me."

AnnMaria De Mars with daughter Ronda Rousey.

Sometimes he'd send me several pages that show something really good and say, "See, you had it wrong in the chapter you sent me. This is how you do that move."

And I would think to myself, "No, this is how you do some other technique. It's very good. But it's not what I was trying to do."

We worked for a few weeks on the mat-work series chapters and they are brilliant. There is no question that the moves Jim described so well in such detail will work for lots of people. I have seen Ronda Rousey, Kayla Harrison, Jimmy Pedro Jr. and others do those exact same mat-work series on many people at a very high level, and they have been very successful. At the same time, as I was reading it, I thought, "If this was my training program, I would hate judo."

In fact, when I was younger, my coach, Jimmy Martin, did a lot of these same series, like the tie-up series. He tried to get me to learn them. It's a great idea. Jimmy Martin won lots of matches doing these techniques, as did Tony Mojica, Dawn Beers and many others from our club who won national and international medals. At some point, I told my coach, "I hate this $#@! and I'm never going to do it. I just hate this."

After really thinking about it over the past year while we wrote this book, I believe the big difference between the way Jim Pedro does judo and the way I do it is that his is very methodical and predictable. That is not a bad thing. Watching Ronda and Jimmy Jr. over the years, there have been many times in a match when I knew they had it won because they had passed the point of no return. That is, they had gotten far enough into a series of steps that the only possible end was for the opponent to be turned and armbarred.

A few months after Ronda's world title fight, I finally had a chance to watch it. When she was pulling Miesha Tate over on the final armbar, my husband (who knows about as much about judo as I know about crochet, that is, he knows how to spell it) said, "That was the point where I knew she had it."

So, no, predictable is definitely not bad.

Yet ... there is another way of doing judo, and that is what I do. In preparing this book for publication, the photographers shot many, many drills during practice. After we had selected the drills and techniques we wanted to use, Ronda, Travis McLaughlin and Crystal Butts went to the *Black Belt* studios and its photographer shot high-quality photos of the same moves. When I was looking through all the pictures that Jim said were wrong, I noticed a couple of things. He was correct in that the reaction of the opponent varied from picture to picture. He was right when he said, "Once in a great while, the person might move his or her arm out like that to stop a half nelson, but maybe only one time out of a hundred."

And yet, in almost all those pictures, I was armbarring someone. And, in almost all those pictures, they were *not* posed. That is, I would try a half nelson, and whatever the person did, I would go into an armbar. So they obviously *did* put their arm out. (Why, they'll surely starve to death except for the odd exceptionally lucky one here and there.)

When I was competing, it was a big joke among my teammates and me about how often articles written after events would report that someone else was favored but "AnnMaria got lucky and won."

There are three differences between Jim and me in our training and competing.

1. He sets people up to provoke a specific move. For example, he will pull in the opponent's wrist to control it, setting him up to pull the arm up allowing space for a half nelson. I, on the other hand, react to whatever the person does. That is, if she puts her right arm out at all, even for a second, I am going to jump on it and do a *juji gatame*. I may fall backward. I may turn toward her hips. I am going to improvise based on whatever my opponent does. Jim plans. I react. Both ways require *a lot* of practice because, as Jim pointed out, for my way to work, I need to anticipate what the opponent is going to do. His way requires lots and lots of practice of the same few moves. My way requires lots and lots of practice of different moves. I would be bored to death executing judo his way, but for some people, it is just wonderful. There are people who hate the way I teach judo. They find it very confusing. They want to be told what to do. They think that as an instructor, I ought to be able to tell them what to do in a given situation and give them a plan that if they follow it long enough and train hard enough, they will win.

2. My way generally requires that you be faster than your opponent. That is, I grab the arm before he or she can react. Because I have practiced thousands of times being in that exact position (and my opponent probably has not), I am usually faster even when the other person has more natural speed than me.

3. In my method, it helps if you are stronger than your opponent. For example, there is a rolling turnover (perhaps a topic for our next

book) I perform. If you have enough strength to reach up, grab your opponent's *gi* and roll him head over heels—or at least get close enough that he reacts by sticking out an arm to stop it—that helps.

Because of those last two points, the "reaction drills" that I teach work more for trainers who are young and fit. For this reason, a lot of older instructors won't like them. I will be the first to admit that I am nowhere near as good as when I was younger. On many techniques, I don't have the power to force them through that I did when I was younger. I'm fine with that. Judo is an Olympic sport. I bet whoever won the Olympics in the 100 meters in 1984 can't run it nearly as fast now, either.

One reason (of many) I like mat work is that strength is more of a factor in it than in standing techniques. If you are stronger than most people, which I almost always was in competition, then it is to your advantage to be in situations in which strength matters most.

Jim's very methodical way of teaching and training mat work is good because it works for a wide range of people, and as someone who has coached for many years, that is what he needs to do.

Most of my life, I have only had to worry about two athletes: Ronda and me. My way might work for the top 10 percent in natural athletic ability. There is nothing wrong with using your strength and athleticism, if you have it. Jim's way works for more people because it does not rely on natural athleticism. However, if you have it, use it. That is, if you are stronger or faster than most people, why on earth would you not want to use that in competition?

My point—and you may have given up by now on me ever having one—is that winning and coaching are intensely personal. You don't have to pick a single technique or even philosophy. That's why we have included so many pages of mat-work techniques and so many coaching tips in this book.

Try them.

Experiment.

Keep what works for you, your strengths and your personality. As we've said several times by now, if you win, it was right—for you.

—AnnMaria De Mars